Should You Stay or Should You Go

*When Marriages Aren't Working: An Inspiring
Personal Story of a Couple Who Found Happiness
When God Brought Them Together Following
Their Difficult Decisions to Divorce*

KIRK AND DEBORAH TAYLOR

WESTBOW
PRESS®
A DIVISION OF THOMAS NELSON
& ZONDERVAN

WestBow Press books may be ordered through booksellers or by contacting:

WestBow Press
A Division of Thomas Nelson & Zondervan
1663 Liberty Drive
Bloomington, IN 47403
www.westbowpress.com
844-714-3454

ISBN: 978-1-6642-5092-5 (sc)
ISBN: 978-1-6642-5091-8 (hc)
ISBN: 978-1-6642-5093-2 (e)

Library of Congress Control Number: 2021925860

Print information available on the last page.

WestBow Press rev. date: 01/04/2022

Introduction

Should You Stay Or Should You Go is the personal story of Kirk and Deborah Taylor. They talk about their childhood experiences and how these experiences shaped them to be who they are as adults. Both were in long term difficult marriages. Kirk was married forty-three years and Deborah was married thirty-five years. They describe their struggles with being Christians as they stayed in their marriages and tried to repair their marriages. They both wanted to honor God but were dying emotionally and eventually were each only married on paper, not in their hearts. This culminated with both of them leaving their marriages at separate times as they sought God's peace and joy. God brought them together after Deborah had been divorced eleven years and Kirk was in the last stages of his divorce. This book is for those who are struggling in a difficult marriage and are trying to decide what steps to take next. It is the hope of the Taylors that the readers can be honest about their situation in order to either repair the marriage or decide to leave the marriage. They believe that God needs to be involved in either decision. He has blessed their marriage together as they walk in His guidance of what He has designed marriage to be. This is how the story begins.

There once was an adventurous ten-year-old boy named Kirk who lived in Utah. He was fascinated with the water and would ride on the city bus at age ten for thirty-five minutes each way to the local Athletic Club to take swimming lessons. One summer, his parents took him to the ocean in Florida. He fell in love with the bright sun, rolling waves, and watching the surfers. Back home he practiced skim boarding at a local man-made lake that had a beach. He broke his leg skim boarding there. He thought skim boarding was sort of like surfing in that it involved a board and water, but he dreamed of the ocean. Seeing it for the first time had made a deep impression on him. It was in the 1960's. The Beach Boys were singing songs about surfers and about surfer girls. A few years later, he found out that he and his family were moving to Florida, near the beach. He mowed lawns and shoveled snow to save money for a surfboard. The first thing he did when he arrived in Florida was to go and buy a surfboard. He walked two blocks to a local surfboard shop, asked what board was good to learn on and bought it. It was blue and white, a used one, but in good condition. He immediately headed down to the ocean and asked the older surfers how to get up on the board. His passion for surfing began.

Around the same time, in southern Idaho, there was a young girl named Deborah who dreamt about surfer dudes and imagined how wonderful it would be to be a surfer girl. She would listen to Wolf Man Jack on her transistor radio every evening at 8:30 p.m. She closed her eyes and visions of boys with sun bleached hair surfing in California would appear as she listened to the Beach Boy's songs. To be a little surfer girl would be the ultimate dream. Loving the water, she spent every summer at a nearby lake with long days at the beach swimming and sunbathing. Her skin became golden brown, and her brunette hair had streaks of gold. She was the captain of the family ski boat and spent most mornings boating and pulling her sisters and friends over the cold, blue waters on water skis. She wondered how it would be in California as a California girl.

How these two people ended up together fifty years later was an act of God. He wove their lives together into one that brought them to Hawaii, where Kirk is a surfer dude and Deborah is a surfer girl. This is their story.

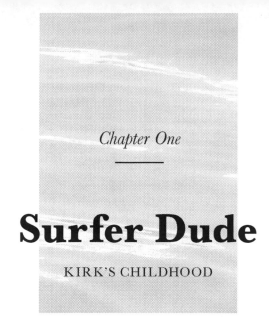

Chapter One

Surfer Dude

KIRK'S CHILDHOOD

I was born in Phoenix, Arizona. A long way from any ocean, seeing that I am a surfer. And you are correct; there are no waves in Phoenix, nor in Utah, the places I grew up until I was fifteen. My dad was in the newspaper business and was transferred a few times as I was growing up. We ended up in Utah where I lived until age fifteen. So, I was born in Phoenix, moved briefly to Louisiana when I was about two, and ended up in Utah at around age three or four. The Louisiana humidity was not a good fit for my parents. There was still no ocean in Utah, but I would eventually get there!

I had a great childhood in Utah in the years that I can remember. I don't remember much of Phoenix and Louisiana, although I do have a vivid memory of my grandfather holding me in his arms and showing me all of the tools in his workshop at probably around eighteen months old. I do not remember Louisiana at all; I think it was too humid for my mind to function very well at that young age.

My Childhood was great up until the eighth grade, and

then there were some real family challenges. My folks went into bankruptcy twice that I remember. One time, our furniture was repossessed. I was at home, sick with a serious chest cold and sleeping on the sofa in the living room when the "haul away guys" arrived to take the sofa I was sleeping on. I will never forget that. It made a lifelong impression on me, and I believe helped me be very frugal with money. From a totally rotten experience, I learned an extremely valuable life lesson.... don't get into too much debt!

My mom was an exceptional mother. She raised me and my sister in a loving, supportive and instructional way. We learned good manners, and she made sure we played sports. She taught me how to cook, as I was always hungry and hanging around the kitchen around dinner time, and I absorbed quite a bit of her talents. I was always tasting things to abate my hunger too. She would feign being irritated, but I think she loved having me hang around and taste her cooking. There was always a little smile that accompanied the admonition to keep my hands out of the food. I am not nearly as good a cook as she was. She taught me how to sew a little also; how to put a button on a shirt, patch a small tear, and even how to use a sewing machine a little. My sister skied, and I played little league. I had piano and guitar lessons. I fell in love with the guitar, and still play it and the piano also. I only wish I had stayed with the lessons longer, as Mom thought I should. I would be a better player today if I had. Sorry, Mom, for not listening, but thanks a bunch for getting me started in music. I am grateful for that.

I think I got some of my handy man abilities from my mom, via her father. He was a tool and die maker. I have some tools he had made, and I shared the memory of him showing me all the tools in his tool shed. He came to America from Poland when he was nineteen years old, in the late 1800s. His family had sent him to America as I guess things were not great in Poland at that time.

I have a picture of him on the deck of the ship, and the menu they served on the ship. When he arrived in New York, he was scammed out of all his money. He was nineteen, and in a new country, with no money. Yet he made it! In the picture you can see a bit of feistiness in his face - not wild, but spunky for sure.

My mom was always the handy person around the house, fixing little things that broke, and I learned from watching and helping her. I remember my sister and I helped her paint our bedrooms in grade school which was fun. I got to use a brush and a roller. The roller was the cool part. My grandfather was also musical and played the zither. My mom shared stories of how he would play, and everyone would sit around and listen. I think he was quite good at it. My mom got that talent and so did I. I am so glad that part got into my genes. It has also gone down to my son and grandsons.

My mom was from my grandfather's second marriage. His first wife had died young after giving birth to her third child. All of my mom's siblings were about ten to twelve years older than her. My grandmother only had my mom, and no other children. I think my mom was the apple of my grandfather's eye, from all that she shared. She adored her father and spoke so lovingly about how fun he was and his musical talents. My cousins said he was a great guy, but strict also. That seemed like a good balance.

I remember one day I had little league practice and I was to play in a piano recital that night. I was playing second base that day. In practice I was talking to another player when the catcher threw the ball to me. I didn't hear him yell "coming down". The ball hit me in the nose, knocked me down and out for a few seconds. I remember my mom coming to get me. The nosebleed had stopped by then. I said, "Do I still have to play at the recital tonight?" The answer was yes! She was committed to my music. I was actually feeling ok but was looking for a way out of the recital because it made me so nervous to play in front of other people. I think this type of experience ingrained in me the pattern and attitude of "don't quit, keep going" no matter what.

We had horses, my favorite thing at that age. I could ride my bike to the stables at one point, a real special childhood memory. Trail riding on the outskirts of town was a special treat. I was about twelve to fourteen years old at this time. My friends and I would ride out to a small restaurant where they had old time hitching posts for the horses. Cars came in from the other side. We would hitch the horses and go inside for some food. I felt like a real cowboy! These types of experiences developed my early independence.

Mom took us to church often. She had an inner curiosity or hunger for God, which developed in later years into her salvation and knowing Jesus as her personal Savior. We went from Presbyterian, to Methodist, to Episcopal during my growing up years. I remember being scared to death as an altar boy in the Episcopal Church because of the robes and scepters of the priests. In none of these churches did anyone ever introduce me to Jesus or ask if I knew Him as Savior. But mom introduced us to God the best she knew how.

My dad loved to fish the rivers in the mountains, so he taught me how to fish. I loved it. I would practice casting in the back yard for hours, and eventually graduated to fly casting. That was challenging, but fun when I finally could keep the line in the air until I had released enough to set the fly down where I wanted. We would drive to the mountains for the weekend, stay in a small cabin somewhere, and fish. I would get up early in the morning, walk out by myself at around age ten or eleven, and fish until lunch, "working the river" as my dad had taught me; walking up and down for quite a spell in each direction. Many times, I was all alone, with no one else around. I loved the beauty of nature, the flowing water in the river and the calm pools. The pine trees, meadows and grasslands were inspiring to me. Catching a fish on my own was very exciting and I felt great when I got a few before lunch. Fishing alone helped develop my sense of confidence, self-assuredness and independence. Something that became part of who I am. Even when Dad was with me, we would always keep a good space between us, as we were working different parts of the river. Sometimes we were on opposite sides of the river if there was a place to cross over. And then it was really great when one of us would tell the other, "I got one!"

Nothing seemed to smell or taste as good as my mom's cooking in the mountains! She was a great cook to begin with, but there was something about that fresh mountain air that seemed to multiply the amazing smells of her cooking. After fishing in the afternoon, as I was walking back to our cabin, I would be greeted by the aromas of a delicious meal being prepared, and by then I was really hungry! Boy did it smell good.

A couple of times when the fishing was not really good, or later in the afternoon, my folks would let me go tubing down the river. I would sit in the inner tube and push out into the current. I had no life vest or flotation other than the inner tube. It was a blast! My folks would pick me up downstream a little as I remember. How did we survive the stuff we were allowed to do? We even survived being hit by the "dodge ball" without significant emotional trauma from being eliminated from the game.

My dad was always a happy soul. No matter how difficult the prior day had been, he would wake up with a smile and in a good mood. Maybe his tough years growing up taught him to find happiness where he was and not let the events of life keep you down. His father had been killed in a tree trimming accident on their farm in Missouri when my dad was about five or six years old. He was riding on horseback, checking on the trimming, when a limb hit him in the head and killed him. My dad and several of his siblings lived in an orphanage for a while until his mom could get things together. There were seven kids. He worked from a very young age, and just never complained about much of anything. I recall him sharing how he worked on an ice truck, delivering ice as a very young kid. He loved to joke around and make you laugh. He did not have a lot of time to support me in sports or after school events. I remember on a few occasions he would play catch with me with a hard ball. I still remember how fun that was for me. He did show up for some of my ball games. He helped me learn how to play golf too. But that was a sport I never connected with. I think because my dad never really had a father growing up, being an engaged father did not come naturally to him.

I think I learned the love of nature from my folks. They were always sharing the beauty around us as we would drive through the country, or in the mountains, commenting to each other and to us about what they saw; a field of tall standing corn, or a beautiful stretch of river, or a meadow. I did that same thing with my kids and grandkids. I am grateful to them for instilling in me an appreciation for the beauty of God's creation. Sometimes on a weekend afternoon we would simply go for a drive in the country. Our town wasn't all that big back then, and within a short while we were in the corn fields. We had a couple of BBQ restaurants we would stop at for dinner after a scenic drive. That was always fun! The purpose of the drive was to enjoy the views of the countryside and have a nice family meal. I still remember this one place that had the best BBQ ribs which were served with these really wide curled carrots. I was so curious of how they made them curl. I'm not sure how they did that, but I still can picture how they looked on the plate. These were really positive family times.

My dad worked a great deal, so I did not have much weekly interaction with him other than at dinner, a meal we almost always shared together. He took me to work with him on a few occasions. He showed me the printing presses at the newspaper where he worked, and once he took me with him on a Saturday morning to distribute advertising throw away weekend papers. The newspaper would distribute these by giving a bundle to the homeless folks, and others down on their luck, to pass out around the downtown area. I think my dad had to handle this distribution sometimes when someone didn't show up for work, because he was the Advertising Manager for the paper.

He always bought me firecrackers and M-80s for the fourth of July. Probably deemed as an irresponsible thing to do, but I thought it was great. He offered some words of caution about them, and how you could get really hurt, and then gave them to me. The M-80s were pretty powerful little explosives. They sure made a huge bang, at least to me as a kid. Sometimes a friend and I would sneak out at night, after our folks were asleep, and blow up a few around the neighborhood. We were stealthy enough to not get caught, and never did damage any property. There was something very satisfying about completing our mission undetected and returning home. My self-confidence was bolstered by our secret success! There was a pattern in my growing up developed by being allowed to experience things on my own; to be alone along a river, ride horses out for a lunch with my friends and secret "night missions". These repeated themselves and developed good qualities in me such as independence, self-assuredness, confidence and the like. Thanks, Mom and Dad for letting me grow up this way!

One day my dad came home with a pink Cadillac for my mom. I remember the tail fins on that thing; they were huge! I don't remember how old I was for sure, but I was around eleven or twelve, I think. One day we were up in the mountains for a drive, and I asked to please be able to drive the car. My dad took us to a remote dirt road area with flat ground on both sides of it. He let me drive! I could barely see over the huge Cadillac steering wheel. I remember hitting the gas too hard, then the brake, and trying to not forget to steer. I had a great time! And we managed to stay on the road.

Another time we went sledding in the foothills after a fresh snow fall. We had a sled which was made of wooden slats on metal rails, and a cross bar up front which let you steer it a little, but not really. You could pull and push that cross bar with all of your strength and not change the direction of the sled. You laid on your stomach to ride it. Well, they set me loose down the hill and away I went. However, I went to fast and too far, right into a barb wire fence which went across my nose. Some blood, but no serious injury. I am not sure my folks noticed the fence, or if they did, they must have thought I wouldn't get that far.

My dad and mom had friends in the newspaper business. They owned a chain of newspapers. They were quite wealthy. I remember visiting their home in Naples, Florida which had a sixteen-car garage with antique cars, a museum in their basement of items collected from their world travels, and a ninety-foot yacht in the harbor. One summer they bought an old yellow school bus and drove it out to Utah to visit my folks, just for the fun of it. We went to the mountains for a day drive in the school bus. It was so much fun! I remember at lunch my dad and his old friend were having beer with their burgers. I asked my dad if I could taste the beer. He said sure, but don't let the waitress see you. That was my first taste of beer, and I felt like a man among men!

My dad and my mom had a great work ethic. They always dug back in and kept working, even through bankruptcy. And my dad always worked, even after he retired many years later. This must have added to my work ethic because I have always been a hard worker. I find great satisfaction in working diligently in anything I put my hands to.

I learned the value of work when I was in grade school, raking leaves and shoveling snow for folks around our neighborhood. It always felt good to have earned my own money to buy a few things. And I could ride my bike two blocks to a cool little store that had some of my favorite things. That meant new steely marbles, a game we always played at school, candy, or these really cool bird whistles made of a small piece of leather and some very thin cellophane type material. You would get the leather wet, put it in your mouth in a certain way, and they could really produce a loud whistle. I am sure someone choked on those things, as you sure won't find them around today. I learned my work ethic from my folks, and for that I am grateful.

When I was in about fourth grade, there was the beginning of alcohol abuse starting with my mom, and to some degree, my dad. He would not drink during the week, but on weekends he would sometimes come home from a poker game with his friends really drunk. I don't know how he drove home, but he did.

My mom was more of a closet drinker- literally. I remember finding small bottles of hard liquor in her closet…. kids are snoopy you know. I remember throwing some away a few times, because when she drank things were just not the same. Her drinking at this point was not terrible but bothered me enough to try and stop it by throwing the bottles away.

One night when I was about thirteen years of age, my parents had both been drinking heavily. They got into a very heated argument with high volume screaming at each other, and I was afraid someone was going to get hurt. I took a large kitchen knife, held it pointed up in the air and screamed at them, "Stop it!" They did. I guess this led the way to my behavior later in life where I would stand between my ex-wife and our children in arguments to protect them as she would be out of control screaming at them. I became the fixer of things. Deborah, my wonderful current wife, who has a master's degree in counseling, tells me that this is common behavior for a person who takes the role of being the one who steps in to fix problems between others.

Meanwhile – Deborah was growing up in eastern Oregon. A high desert area with mountains, valleys, sagebrush, and a few trees. There was no ocean, and the lake was many miles away.

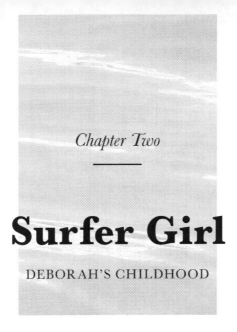

Chapter Two

Surfer Girl

DEBORAH'S CHILDHOOD

I grew up in a family with five daughters, and one brother – I am the oldest. Well, not really five children as my parent's first child died at birth so I never knew her. I only knew that her name was Cindy. My folks never talked about it, as I think it was too painful for them. My father was from a ranching family in eastern Oregon. His grandparents were pioneers. Their ranch was on the stagecoach and wagon train routes. My mother grew up in a small town in Western Oregon of several hundred people. She was of Spanish and Scotch Irish heritage. Her name was Catherine.

Catherine met my father, John, at a dance in a small rural town. He was a rancher, and they owned a ranch in Oregon when I was born. I was the first born who survived, and my mother cried when she saw me. She said I looked like an Indian baby. Their next daughter, Paula, was born fourteen months after me. The winter she was born was the worst in known history and many of the cattle died during the winter due to the freezing cold and deep snow. A ranch hand had accidentally set the haystack on fire the previous fall, leaving my father with not enough hay to feed the cattle over the hard winter. The roads were blocked, and hay could not be brought in. The state started an Arial hay lift for the ranches to drop hay in for the cattle, but it was too late to save most of the cattle and calves. My father was working twenty hours a day and the losses were devastating.

We then moved to another nearby community for a year, while my father leased out the ranch trying to save it. He worked as a security guard and then ended up as manager of a local feed store. Sadly, he lost the ranch.

I have few memories of that time. I have just a vague memory of being in a field with my dad at the ranch. He would put me in the manure pile so I could dig out worms and play with them. That must be why I love bugs to this day (but not worms)!!! I remember being puzzled when the worms would crawl away, and I couldn't find them. I once saw some water snakes and excitedly told my dad that I wanted to catch the big worms. My father often tells the story of when he took me with him to a field at the edge of the ranch and I threw the truck keys into some tall grass. He had a long walk back to the house with a two-year-old in tow!

After my parents lost the ranch, we moved again to another town in northeastern Oregon, as my father decided to sell real estate. We lived in a two-bedroom house and two more siblings were born, Bob and Shelli. I was five and a half when Shelli was born. My mother was nervous and prone to fits of temper. My father was calm and unemotional, and he loved to take us out into nature and teach us about the natural world.

I had a mostly happy childhood, but I learned to get quiet when my mother raged and then I would do things to calm her down. When I was six, we moved into a new house they had built. It was the biggest house in town and sat on a hill overlooking the town. My father taught me how to ride horses, and we even had a blue-eyed pony named Blue, we kept in a corral in the back section of the property. I learned to ride the pony. It was magical. I also learned to enjoy the plants, animals, and insects that surrounded me. I remember many hours spent catching butterflies, caterpillars, grasshoppers and lady bugs and enjoying being outside. My sister Paula and I built several brick homes in the back area. They were about six feet by eight feet wide with no roof. They even had a fireplace. We figured out how to interlay the bricks, so the walls were sturdy, about three feet tall! We had beds, a table, and even a pot to pee in, which we actually used. We felt so clever! Once, I got matches, started a fire, and cooked some tomatoes from the neighbor's garden mixed in with dough I had found in my mom's kitchen. Sadly, I got caught cooking with fire one day and my days as a chef were over. The pot we peed in disappeared also! What fun we had in those houses!! My imagination was in full gear as I played in my houses with my sister and friends. I learned to be creative.

There was also a big sand box in the back yard that my dad had made. The cats thought it was their litter box, so when we played in the sand box, we would just throw the cat poop out. No one was too worried about cat poop back then in the 1950's. I also loved to read. The summer between kindergarten and first grade I read a Grimm's Fairy Tale book I found on a bookshelf. I would carefully sound out the words. I had discovered a new world outside of my own! I believed in those fairy tales and knew I would have a prince come and find me someday. (He did show up when I was sixty-four, and his name is Kirk!). My father had built a rock garden where fairies lived (I was one of them) and many imaginary tales of kings, queens, princesses, fairies, and elves were played out in the rock garden. Oh, the wonderful magic of childhood.

I also read comic books. My Grandmother worked at a soda fountain and would give the left-over comic books to me. How I wish I still had them today! I had a cat named Blondie, who had kittens at least once a year. She would hide them until their eyes opened and then she would proudly bring them one by one to the front door. My dog, Candy, would then help take care of the kittens by licking them and mothering them. My imagination and world were full of nature, horses, kittens, cats, dogs, butterflies, birds, fairy tales, and comic book adventures. I got As in school and had lots of friends.

However, not all of my early childhood memories are happy ones. I remember when I was six my mother was sitting on the steps crying. I didn't know why she was crying. But she turned her sadness into anger at me, grabbed my hair, pulled me around in a circle and kicked at me. I remember going into the bathroom, locking the door and thinking I could take all the aspirin and die. (How I knew about aspirin being an overdose, I don't know.) I really wanted to die. But then I remembered that I was invited to a birthday party of a friend in a few days and decided I didn't want to die. I remember having thoughts of dying one other time, but I don't know how old I was. I developed a twitch in my neck around this time probably due to the anxiety and stress I was experiencing as a young child due to my mother's outbursts. These were signs of depression, anxiety, and perhaps trauma. Since I was the oldest of five children, I became a bit of a caretaker of my younger siblings and also in a way a caretaker for my mother as I tried and keep her calm and protect my younger siblings from her wrath. She was emotionally abusive and also slapped me a lot. It caused me to be very insecure.

I recently learned that my mom was suffering from postpartum depression at the time she attacked me when I was six years old. Now I understand more of her behavior. Later in that year we went to a lake several hundred miles away for three weeks in the summer and she had sessions with a psychiatrist in a town nearby.

I'm not sure what transpired with the psychiatrist but maybe that helped her with the depression. That visit began her love affair with the lake, which she handed down to all of us kids. We then started to go to the lake every summer for a few weeks.

I think my mom had Post Traumatic Stress Disorder (PTSD) also. Her parents divorced when she was four and she witnessed physical and verbal abuse on both their parts. She saw her father throw her mother into a shower of very hot water. She barely spoke for a year after their divorce. She was also in a car accident when she was nineteen. On a rainy night she was driving on a two-lane road in northern Oregon. A truck came over the line headed straight for her. She turned the car to the right to avoid the truck. Her uncle, who was asleep in the passenger seat woke up, grabbed the wheel and turned it straight into the truck, head on. The other driver died, and my mom was injured with a broken nose and other injuries. Her uncle was also injured. It was hours before another car came along to help. She never got over the accident emotionally and carried guilt thinking she had caused it. "Post-Traumatic Stress Disorder is based in experiencing a physical injury, severe emotional or mental distress or a life-threatening event." "What is PTSD", American Psychiatric Association, accessed on November 7, 2021. https://www.psychiatry.org/patients-families/ptsd/what-is-ptsd

What was the result of my mother's Depression and PTSD? She was very anxious and upset a good part of the time. Her functioning as a parent was impaired in many ways. She was not able to support me emotionally as she was herself unstable emotionally at times. An example of this is she would make statements that she never really wanted children. She also said, "What you don't have, you don't miss." I felt I was in the way many times. She made it clear that to have children was a burden to her and it exhausted her. All throughout my young life, when my mom got upset at me, she would threaten to send me away to boarding school. This would terrify me. These messages also got into my psyche. They played out later when my ex-husband would threaten to leave me to get his way. This set me up to respond to threats of being abandoned by becoming conciliatory and docile.

When I was nine, my youngest and the fifth sibling, Heidi was born. I was thrilled as I loved babies. I helped take care of her, holding her and feeding her the bottle whenever I could. I even got up in the night with her and changed her diapers and gave her the nighttime bottle starting when she was three months old or so. My mother let me be the child mother.

This set me up for future caretaking of my siblings and others as an adult. I have felt responsible for my younger siblings my whole life, until recently. To calm and soothe my mother, I learned to accept her out of control screaming, which developed into an unhealthy pattern of behavior for me. These patterns of experiencing verbal abuse and then using tactics to calm the unstable person down are patterns that I carried into my first marriage and other relationships for most of my adult life.

My spiritual life started when I was in first grade. My mother was Catholic, and I had been baptized Catholic. I went to Catechism and learned about God and Jesus. A nun taught the classes. My Mom thought I was going to be a nun because I was so intrigued and excited about God. I heard about the Ten Commandments and that stealing is a sin. I had stolen some candy a few months earlier with a friend who showed me how to do it. My little conscience was so stricken that I had sinned! I was beside myself. I vowed never to steal again. The nun taught that if a person wasn't a Catholic, they would go to Hell. You could only go to Heaven if you were a Catholic. I went to school and told all the non-Catholic kids that they were going to Hell! My mother was so upset that she left the church and we started going to the other church in town – the Methodist church (my dad's church). I was devastated when the Catholic kids told me that I was now the one going to Hell, and that the Priest had even said it. This being because I wasn't going to the Catholic church! Boy – was I frightened! My mother assured me this wasn't so. She had some Christian discernment at that time, and she was searching for God herself.

When I was eight, I went to a summer's week of Vacation Bible School. A lady had come to the Methodist church to teach it. I think she went around to the smaller towns of Oregon to teach the Vacation Bible School. She told us about Jesus – that Jesus is Love. I asked him into my heart that summer. My encounters with God were very important to me. I had a babysitter tell me I needed to ask Jesus into my heart also. I told my dad and he said that wasn't necessary as you just needed to go to church and be a good person. He was in error. But I had asked Jesus into my heart and He kept His hand on me from then on.

My mother's mental state deteriorated slowly over time. My fourth sister, Shelli was a wanderer, and my mother didn't pay attention to where she was. Several times, I was sent out into the sagebrush to find my little sister, and I would find her sitting in a pile of red ants as they crawled all over her and bit her. She liked to pick up the ants. I would rush her back to the house where she spent hours in pain. She was three years old. Another time, she wanted to go to the lake, where we had been that previous summer. The lake is a five-hour drive from where we lived but she thought it was close by. She also wanted to see our aunt, who had been at the lake with us. Shelli put on her bathing cap and took off into the sagebrush mountain behind our house. She was dragging her yellow sweater, carrying a new kitten, and the cat Blondie and dog, Candy, followed her. My mother finally noticed she was missing and called and asked for the neighbors and the police to look for her. Hours later, a policeman found her miles away from the house.

When I was eleven, in 1962, we moved again to a larger town. I had to leave behind my friends, my house, my pony, my cat and my childhood. We moved because my mother had several fights with some of her friends in town. My mother was very social but insecure. She was a fabulous hostess and gave beautiful dinner parties and gatherings. She also was very proud of her table manners. This was drilled into me, and I appreciate that she passed this down to me. But when she became upset or angry, she would tear verbally into other people in the community, and it was time to move out of the town.

I became very shy when we moved and had difficulty making friends. My mother would despair when I tried to talk to her about what I was going through and would ask me, "What is wrong with you?" From her response I was sure that I was defective and "less than". I was actually just the new kid at school, but my mother did not know how to explain that to me.

I was often in charge of my younger siblings, and I spent a lot of energy keeping my mother calm. She eventually started drinking excessively when I was thirteen. I was still very insecure and quiet, even though I was a straight A student. I was in the gawky stage with glasses, braces, a headgear and pimples. My acne was a big problem for me, and I would cover it with make-up. My parents didn't think to take me to a doctor. My Mom blamed the pimples on what I ate (peanut butter) and not washing my face enough. Oh – those pimples could hurt when they got inflamed! She got me a steamer for my face and finally found Queen Helene's Green Mint Mask! The mint mask did the trick. I would wear it at night. Can you picture me with my mint mask, glasses, braces, a head gear, and rollers in my hair! I was a sight!!! Yes – I curled my hair with rollers and slept in them all night. (When I was little, my mom curled my hair every night and covered the pin curls with a pair of underwear. – this had to be the source of my insecurities!)

A story that is funny now is about milk. My brother, Bob, did not like to eat many foods, especially meat. Our mealtimes were focused on our parents trying to make him eat his dinner. (It was a great way for the child to get attention.) My mother would pour the left-over milk back into the carton for the next meal. At dinner one night, I took a big gulp of milk and was horrified to find food in it! It was potatoes that my brother had spit into his milk glass the night before so he would not have to eat them!!! Gross! My mother stopped pouring the unused milk back into the carton. I can still feel the yucky potatoes in my mouth!

Transgenerational patterns are patterns that are handed down through the generations. Some of them are healthy and some of them are unhealthy. One pattern that was being handed down to me was that someone could yell at you and tear you down but that after it was over, you were supposed to forget that it happened and go back into relationship with that person as if it never happened. This is called the abuse cycle. This consists of some abuse (emotional, mental, or physical) and then a period of honeymoon (Everything is OK, I love you), a period of calm and then a tension building period leading to more abuse. "Understanding the Cycle of Abuse", Healthline, accessed on November 7, 2021. https://www.healthline.com/health/relationships/cycle-of-abuse

I was taught that after someone emotionally demeaned me, then I must pretend that everything was OK. Things would calm down. Then tension would then build again until some more personal attacks would occur. A honeymoon period would occur, and nothing would really change until the tension built up again. Unfortunately, since I was the target of the abuse, I learned to stay quiet until things calmed down. I did not like the conflict and would do everything I could to calm the abuser down, who was usually my mother. This is the coping mechanism that I used.

My teenage years were soon to begin. Kirk was one year ahead of me and his had begun in 1963.

Chapter Three

Surfer Dude

KIRK'S TEENAGE YEARS

By the time I was fourteen, my mom's drinking began to worsen and eventually led to serious alcoholism. When I was a senior in High School, she would sometimes be drunk by ten in the morning. I remember being terribly embarrassed with her drinking, and didn't want friends to come to the house, especially in the evening for sure. It was ugly to observe. When I was twenty, I had become a Christian and did pray hard for her, my dad, and my sister. Soon after that, my mom accepted Jesus as her savior, and was instantly free from her drinking problem (except for one short relapse I will tell you about). It was a beautiful miracle. In one day, it was over, and she was a new person. Just weeks before she came to know the Lord as her Savior, she had confided in me that sometimes she felt like walking out into the ocean to be free from her inner pain. She would say, "I feel like just walking out into the ocean and not stopping." She had reached bottom, and from here the Lord lifted her up out of total despair when she asked Him into her heart. Then, a few weeks later my dad and my sister received the Lord also. In case you're wondering, you will read below how I came to Him first. God was determined to get His loving hands on our family, and He did!

There was one episode after mom accepted the Lord which was terrible. She had flown to see her mom. I was to pick her up at the airport. I was going to drive around the traffic circle at the airport until she came out for her ride home. I drove around until one time I noticed a woman laying on a bench which looked like her. I parked by the curb and went over to her. It was my mom, and she was totally passed out from too much to drink. I felt terrible inside. I carried her to the car and took her home. That was the last time she ever drank. All of this alcohol abuse caused me to never want to drink. And I didn't for many years, not even a glass of wine with dinner. I had never learned how to enjoy wine with a meal, because the only thing I ever learned about alcohol was to hide it, overuse it, and abuse it. It took many years for me to break out of this and learn to enjoy wine with dinner. God has a way of healing us in ways we don't even recognize.

Finally, I was at the ocean! It happened at age fifteen when my parents moved to be near my dad's sisters in Florida. He was from a family of seven kids. As I mentioned, his father had been killed on their farm in Missouri when he was only four or five years old. His father was on horseback, on his farm, riding to check on some tree cutting they were doing, when a limb fell and hit him in the head. I think that he died right there. My grandmother raised all seven of them by herself. She was always called Mama Taylor. My dad and a couple of the younger siblings had to stay in an orphanage for a while right after his dad passed away. The siblings, (two boys and five girls) had learned to help each other after their dad died, and when my folks hit hard times in Utah, two of his sisters and his brother invited them to Florida. My dad had helped them get started in the real estate business years before.

When I learned of the move to Florida, I immediately started investigating surfing. I cannot explain why, but I was in love with the idea of that sport. I had learned to swim really well at the local Athletic Club, taking the bus to lessons on my own at times. I was about ten to eleven years old when I did this, and the Athletic Club was close to downtown as I remember. I was allowed to learn independence at an early age, taking the bus all by myself. My mom had showed me where the pickup and drop off locations were for the public bus line. I loved being in the water. Deborah says I am part fish. I could not wait to get to Florida. I remember practicing skim boarding in Utah at a man-made freshwater lake with a sand beach. I fractured my leg after being hit by my friend's board one day. He fell off and his board came flying into my leg at full speed. It cracked the bone. Skim boarding was not the same as surfing, but it was standing on a board while sliding over shallow water. This was close enough for a kid from Utah now dreaming of riding real waves.

The first week I was in Florida, I bought a surfboard, with money I had saved from odd jobs like raking leaves, shoveling snow for the neighbors, and a part time paper route. I went to the beach and started watching and asking guys how to surf. It became a love affair! I think I was born to be in the ocean. Now, at age seventy-one, I still surf! In fact, I just ordered a new nine-foot four-inch longboard from a great shaper on Oahu. A perfect board for the waves I now play on in the ocean.

I started going to Hawaii in the summers during high school when I was fifteen years old. I would save my money all year to afford staying in Hawaii for the summer. My friends and I lived in our car, camping out. Sometimes we rented rooms and old houses as we could afford. If the surf was flat, we would explore the island, hiking up streams and waterfalls, and exploring lava tubes inside Haleakala Volcano, or cliff jumping into the ocean. I remember one time a friend led us into a lava tube that was hidden off the hiking trail on the way to the Hunters Cabin, which was outside the park boundary. We went into this tube quite a distance until it began to end and get smaller as the ceiling became lower. In the dark it seemed like a mile underground, but I am sure it was not that far at all. At the end there was a smooth surface from a lava bubble, and on it was a tortoise shell, surrounded by goat bones in a ceremonial fashion. He took us to a second lava tube that had a remarkably similar display. Pretty cool! An offering to Pele the Volcano goddess?

At one point there were five of us living out of our car. Surfboards on the roof, pineapples in the trunk of the car, and living from day to day on the money we saved for our summer adventures comprised our life. Back then you could camp out on the beach without getting rousted by the police, at least most of the time. That summer we only were asked to move along one night. My childhood in Utah, and the times I was allowed to be independent and learn self-confidence were now playing out in my teen years.

Sleeping on the ground, under the trees and stars was great. If it did rain, we would huddle in the car until it was over. We showered in the daytime at the freshwater showers at some of the beach parks. One night on the beach my friend woke us all up screaming! A large centipede had crawled into his sleeping bag and stung him. Other than centipedes, sleeping on the beach was great at that age.

One time we rented a cabin type room right on the ocean for a few weeks. That was really living "high" and a real treat. During another summer, I was running short on money toward the time I would return home, and food rationing was necessary. Breakfast was oatmeal. Lunch, a white bread sandwich with something in the middle; lunch meat, peanut butter or whatever we could afford. And dinner was white rice with one-third can of Campbell's soup on top. One can of soup lasted three days, or sometimes only two if we splurged. Then, once a week, we would walk down to an all you can eat buffet for dinner. We stayed there a long time and could hardly walk home. Seriously, it hurt to walk we had eaten so much. I never did ask my folks for money but figured out how to stretch what I had. They didn't have anything to give at that point anyway. They were always in very tight financial difficulties.

As I was developing into a surfer dude and becoming independent, Deborah was entering into some difficult teenage years sprinkled with experiences that would prepare her for a lifetime of loving beaches and water.

Chapter Four

Surfer Girl

DEBORAH'S TEENAGE YEARS

The wisdom and guidance I needed as a teenager was not there. My father was busy with his work and his politics. He ran for a state office and lost. He later was elected to the county counsel. His politics took time away from the family and caused stress in my mother. My mother took all the political issues personally and very seriously. She experienced pain from the state office defeat and later from the criticism he received being in public office. She was not only critical of herself, my father, other people, but also, she was critical of me. She also was very sensitive to how she was treated socially and if she was being included or not. That included the fact that I was not in the popular crowd, and I disappointed her. I felt inadequate, but I didn't have the social skills to be in the popular crowd.

My father was the opposite. He was positive and let any social or political negativity roll off of him. He created stability in the family when he wasn't busy with work or politics. My father would go to town in his bathrobe and slippers every Saturday to get doughnuts for our breakfast. He made hot chocolate to go with the doughnuts! He also made pancakes on Sunday with our names spelled out or in the shape of animals. Blueberry muffins and mush were also some of his specialties. He made so many things fun for me!

And my father would take us kids on drives and walks often to see what was alive in the world on weekends. He had been a rancher, so he had a horse from the ranch, Sparky. He also bought Blackie, a twenty- six-year-old riding stable horse. Blackie would plod along. If I hit him with the reins he would trot. I never saw him lope! He was a perfect horse for young girls. Sparky was a working Quarter Horse gelding from my dad's ranch. He was a magnificent horse and responded to any command. He was fun to gallop on. My father also bought a donkey named Pepper. Boy, was she stubborn! The horses and Pepper were kept in a field across from the house. When Pepper was first put in the field, all the horses in the field (about twenty of them) chased her for over an hour around and around the field. Finally, an old white horse decided she was to be his friend and he ran the other horses off. They were best friends for the rest of the time. Can you imagine how wonderful it was for me to walk across the street with a bucket of oats and a halter to get a horse or donkey to ride?

When I was fourteen my father gave me, a small Arabian mare named Carmel. She was green broke – which means she wasn't quite rideable. Carmel gave me many wild rides where she would buck, try and roll over on me or push me into a fence. She eventually calmed down but never was totally trustworthy. I spent many hours riding the horses or lying in the horse pasture in the green grass, enjoying the smells, wildflowers, trees, and clouds in the sky. These were my safe havens. When I was upset, I went there to calm down, which was often.

My four siblings have been very important to me since I was a child. Paula is fourteen months younger than me. We were best friend sisters and always shared a room together. She was very pretty and always attracted a lot of attention. We helped each other get through the chaos of the home. Bob is the third and middle child. He was aggressive and wanted to be "firstest". He was my father's favorite. My Dad always took his side and the rest of us were punished if there was a fight (he never was punished). He is four years younger than me. He was and has continued to be an angry, toxic person. He was actually a bully. I remember when I was about thirteen years old, I had had enough. Since we had horses, we all had cowboy boots. Bob would put on his boots and kick me and Paula when our parents weren't around. It really hurt!! Paula and I would complain to our dad, and he would ignore us and believed Bob's stories of denial. One day, our parents were going to be gone for the day. Paula and I decided to pay Bob back. We put on our cowboy boots and kicked him a bunch of times! Oh – that felt great, and it was so much fun to pay him back. He went running out of the house to his friend's house. I can't remember if we got in trouble or not, but we sure didn't care if we did.

The fourth child is Shelli. She was a child of nature and was easy going as a child. She became quite all about herself as a teenager, and this has continued. Heidi is the fifth child. I was her second mother, and she has been a lost child. She was always very to herself and still is. Being as I was the oldest child, I felt I needed to take care of my siblings.

My parents bought a cabin at the lake when I was fourteen, as the lake was now close by. My mother still loved the lake and the beach, and this was a gift to me. I spent whole summers at the lake; boating, swimming, and enjoying the beach. My Dad bought a boat and gave me the keys and a gas credit card! We were a block from the beach and the boat was on a buoy in the bay. My sister and I would get up at 6:00 a.m. and swim to the boat (we had no rowboat). (There were no kayaks in use at the lake at that time). We would swim out to the boat, go to shore, and pick up the other kids and any friends who were visiting, and take them water skiing. I was fourteen and my sister was thirteen!!! We would take turns driving the boat for water skiing and racing around the lake until the waves came up around noon. We would drop everyone off, tie up the boat and swim back in. It was a long swim, and I almost drowned several times. My mother would often stand on the beach and scream at me while giving directions as I drove the boat in and out of the bay.

Then, I would spend the rest of the day at the beach with a towel, baby oil for my gorgeous tan, and lemon juice to bleach my hair blond. These were happy times most of the time. I would drink water out of the lake (no plastic water bottles in those days) and would trudge to the cabin for lunch – barefoot. I have a deep love of a beach, lake, or ocean to this day. We washed our hair in the lake in the evenings (not allowed now) and my sisters and I would go skinny dipping in the lake under the stars and the moon. That is the 1960's for you! Lots of freedom. And simple things for happiness. No internet, cell phones, and no TV in the cabin either.

This sounds like the perfect life for a teenager – right? I had a horse and spent the summers at the lake. I had a boat and got to water ski. I lived in a very nice home. Things can look wonderful from the outside, but often the true life inside a home can be not so wonderful.

As a teenager, I remember lots of times when my mom lit into me. She would rage and would slap me. I would end up in my room sobbing for hours. My father would come in eventually and would then proceed to tell me that I lived in a nice house, had horses, a lake house, a boat, and he was an important man. Therefore, I shouldn't have any problems and I had nothing to complain about so "get out there and apologize to your mother". He taught me that I was responsible for any abuse that came my way. Here I was being abused, verbally and physically, and I was being told to apologize! This was so confusing. My father never protected me from my mother's verbal and sometimes physical abuse. He also never protected me from my brother Bob's aggressive, lying behavior.

I was not a bad teenager, and I don't remember what would precipitate those episodes with my mother. I didn't drink, party, or act out. I was responsible and would help clean the house, do wash, clean the dishes, mow the lawn, babysit, and pull weeds. It was crazy making at its best and affected me for many years. (Crazy making is when a person is told they don't know what they know, don't feel what they feel, don't hear what they hear, don't see what they see and this leads to self-doubt.) This taught me to keep all of my pain and thoughts to myself and to doubt my own feelings and reality. I was not allowed to speak up for myself or to defend myself. I felt I was to blame for the behavior of my mother. And the interactions with Bob left me with a deep hatred of lying behavior. Patricia Evans, *The Verbally Abusive Relationship*, (Adams Media, 2009)

Another incident that stands out when I was a teenager occurred at the cabin at the lake. The cabin was 800 square feet with a bathroom only one person could barely fit into. The cabin was very full, with five kids and at times an extra friend or two. I was fifteen and was the typical teenage girl into make-up and my hair. I had slept in that particular morning, and when I got up everyone was at the beach except my mother. Wow – I could spend some time in the bathroom doing my makeup and hair! I came out looking beautiful after thirty minutes or so. My mother was sitting outside on the stairs. She started screaming at me that I was selfish, and she had been waiting for twenty minutes and needed to use the bathroom! She had never even knocked on the door to let me know she was there. She ripped me to pieces. That popped my balloon on how great I looked with my hair and makeup, as my beautiful make up job ended up on my tear-stained cheeks!!! It was a sneak attack.

I found out later that my mother was on six times the normal dose of progesterone and she was only 39 at the time. The doctor was giving her that for her nervousness and depression instead of what was typically prescribed at the time – valium. Those hormones added to her unstable behavior. But I didn't know it then. I was a very confused, insecure teenager. The overdosing of the hormones later gave her the breast cancer, from which she died.

My mother would get drunk in the evenings. She would stand by the clock watching it until 5:00 p.m. came and then she would start drinking wine. She often said a person is not an alcoholic if they don't drink before 5:00 p.m. By the time we sat down for dinner, she would be drunk. She wouldn't eat, would continue drinking wine and would cry and say she was miserable. She would say she despaired. My Dad didn't say a word as we sat and ate, and she wailed drunkenly about her terrible life. She also had issues with friends and others that she would rant about, which were very blown up out of proportion. Later in the evening she would sit on the couch and pass out. My father never addressed her drunken behavior or her abusive behavior and acted like it was normal. I did not recognize this behavior was "abnormal" and I ignored it like my father did.

The verbally attacks became worse. She was extremely critical of me and anything that I did. An example was when one night I babysat my younger sisters and cleaned the whole house. When my parents came home, my mom saw a Kleenex on the floor that didn't make it to the garbage can. She went on a rampage about how irresponsible I was and how messy the house was. My father did not stop her or defend me --he never did. I went to my room broken hearted to be so accused and not thanked for the clean house. This created in me the mindset that it was my fault when abuse or when my mother lost control occurred, and that I shouldn't talk about it or recognize it. I had lots of guilt feelings, self-blame, and self-doubt. I felt inferior and compensated by being over-responsible.

What about the other parent that doesn't stop the abuse? My father just watched it. He also watched my first husband be extremely verbally and psychologically abusive toward me. My dad never spoke up to say this wasn't normal or acceptable. However, he and my mother bickered constantly. He would argue with her to stop her verbal abuse towards him, but he ignored her behavior toward us children.

My pattern of unhealthy thinking was set.

From the time I was little, I prayed to God and would talk to Him throughout the day. I had a Bible and I read it often. Especially when I was a teenager, I would read the Bible. But when I was seventeen, I rebelled. But before I tell you about it – let's see how Kirk handled his coming into young adulthood at age eighteen.

Chapter Five

——

Surfer Dude

KIRK'S YOUNG ADULTHOOD AND MARRIAGE

Just before my eighteenth birthday, after I graduated from high school, I moved to Hawaii. I got a job in construction and surfed when I wasn't working. I hung doors for a condo project, poured concrete, and worked on a couple of houses from the foundations to the roof. I learned a lot about how houses are built. I remember pouring concrete on Maui, up in Kula for a steep driveway when it started raining. That was a real challenge to keep the "mud" in place until the concrete started to cure. After high school and up until I was twenty, I lived in Hawaii on and off, on Maui in various places. My work was construction and handyman type work, building decks, remodeling a small old home, hanging drywall and painting. I did not like painting and was not very good at it either. We built a pig barn with a concrete floor for the rancher we worked for part time and lived in a shack on his property. We grew potatoes out back once and fried them up the moment we picked them. Wow were they great!

From the bathroom of the shack, you could see both sides of Maui! It was an amazing ocean view! It had a bathroom, a bunk bed area, and a small kitchen. I built the bunk beds for us. I had worked as a carpenter's apprentice for a couple of years so had the basic skills to build stuff. Up to six of us lived there at times. There were several back-and-forth visits to the mainland too. I had a construction job accident, nearly cutting off one finger and damaging another when I was eighteen. The doctor explained that the best option for the most damaged finger was to cut it off at the knuckle. I remember asking the doctor to please try and fix it the best he could without taking it off because I played the guitar. The injury was on my left hand, the hand I used on the neck to play cords and such. He said he would do the best he could and did a pretty good job. It has remained useable, although not the best to play with. I am grateful to have my finger though.

I received a settlement for my injury of a few thousand dollars, which seemed like a million! I recall one splurge with the guys I lived with. I took them to the Kula lodge for blueberry pancakes. They were known for them. I lived off the settlement money for quite a while and bought a Martin D-28 Brazilian Rosewood steel string acoustic guitar before the money was all gone. I still have it today! I could have bought an acre of land in Wailea, which would have been a great investment, but my mind was elsewhere at the time and not at all focused on my financial future. I was drafted to go to Viet Nam shortly after the accident and I flew to Honolulu for my physical thinking I was going to the war. My finger injury prevented them from accepting me, so back to Maui I went. I was relieved. That war did not seem to make any sense at all from what I could understand. I think God spared me from the war, as he had other plans for me.

Watching my parent's struggle financially, in their marriage, and in their drinking brought me to a place of thinking that the only thing that mattered in life was to live and enjoy the moment. You can live, work, struggle, lose everything, be miserable and then it was over.... you died. Seeing how hard they worked, and yet failed, had deflated my opinion of trying to acquire stuff. And this discouraged me from any real goals or ambitions in life other than living for today, having fun, and yes, working hard to have some money. This observation and initial position I took in life actually led to a serious pursuit in my heart of "why am I here and what is the purpose of life"?

From age eighteen to twenty I searched for God. He had placed a hunger in my heart, a yearning which I did not fully understand. I wanted to know who or what He was. Living in Hawaii brought me in contact with some pretty fringe element type folks. Space cadets was a common term for them. Some of them were heavy into drugs, heavy drugs. Others were spacing out on nature or involved with some other religious cult. I think just about every religion or spiritual sect on the planet can be found in Hawaii. At least it seemed I heard about a lot of them. The guys I hung out with did some pot, and drank Primo, the Hawaiian beer. A few got way into heavier stuff. One very gifted surfer got stuck on heroin and ended up dying pretty young. It is a very sad story. He was so fluid in the water, amazing to watch. I dabbled with pot, tried LSD once, but the LSD and the other stuff scared me. God, even then, had His hand on me and kept me safe from getting into anything that would really harm me. While I had learned independence and confidence at an early age, I never did stupid things that would harm me. I took measured risks but was not crazy.

Diverting to a time when I spent some months on the mainland; I had wanted to become an airline pilot. In high school I was fortunate to take ground school as a high school class and got my pilot's license when I was seventeen. The only college that offered pilot training was near my grandmother. One of the other students in my flight class and I lived with her for a few months while attending the college. That didn't last long as the commute was way too long, and my grandmother was too stressed with two young guys living with her. She had been a widow for many years and was accustomed to living alone. Well, this other student turned out to be a pretty big drug dealer, selling stuff to the people who sold it to the users. He attempted to get me into "the business" in a very subtle way, explaining how much money I could make doing what he did. I remember how dark that all sounded and felt, and I wanted no part in it. I did not want to end up in jail for selling kilos of marijuana. God was keeping me even then!

Anyway, back to Maui. I would explore almost anything if I could find out what life's purpose was all about. I read different books, listened to many different schools of thought on the subject and was truly seeking an answer to life's purpose. I tried through diet by eating only live foods for I had read that this was a way to spiritual enlightenment. I didn't find enlightenment but did get skinnier. In fact, real skinny! My intake included banana, pineapple, avocado, nuts and some grains. I would cheat sometimes and put mayonnaise on the avocado. Wow - that was delicious! I think the diet adventure lasted maybe six months and then I became more moderate about it. I had a hunger for God but had not found Him yet. I certainly was putting in an effort to understand the meaning of life, and that quest was His gift to me - to draw me to Himself.

For some reason, the same day I bought my Martin D-28 guitar, I bought a Bible. The bookstore was in the same shopping center as the guitar store. I cannot tell you why, but I did. Somewhere in the back of my mind I think I bought it because of something a friend had shared with me about God, or Jesus or the Bible. Now I can tell you it was the Lord, but I didn't know it then. I started reading in Genesis and read all the way through.

I was not born again, and did not come to Jesus from this alone, but I was reading God's word.

At Christmas, when I was age twenty, my close friend, who had been seeking God with me, had gone back to Florida a few months earlier, attended a prayer fellowship and been born again. He wrote to me, sent me Gospel tracts, and said when I came home for Christmas, I needed to go with him to this fellowship.

When I left Hawaii and went to the mainland for Christmas, I went to the prayer meeting. I sat alone in the back row as my friend cancelled at the last minute. It was the first time anyone ever said I needed to know Jesus personally, and that it was He who had died for my sins and was the only way to God. It was the first time I recall ever hearing that it was Jesus' shed blood that was the only thing that could wash away my sins. I didn't understand all of that very well. Going from seeking spiritual enlightenment by eating avocados to the blood of Jesus cleansing my sins was a quantum leap. I had read the Bible, but the clarity of this Gospel message was new to me.

I went home that night in a bit of a daze but determined to come back in the morning for the Thursday morning service. Something had resonated in my heart, even though I didn't fully understand it. When the time came to ask if anyone wanted to receive Jesus as their Savior, I stared at the preacher (a woman by the way). She looked straight at me and said, "You, son, I feel God is working in your heart." He sure was! With no other words spoken, and no invitation to come forward, I bolted to my feet, walked up to the front by the podium, and there said the sinner's prayer. I felt I had stepped in the right direction. And I began to absorb just a little bit, for the first time in my life, why I was here, and what the purpose of life was! God had found me, and I had found Him. About two weeks later I received the Baptism of the Holy Spirit. That was not a real exciting event. I felt nothing; no tingles, no great revelations, no warmth…. nothing. But I put into practice praying in tongues, singing and worshipping in the Spirit immediately. Things began to really open up for me when I read the Bible. I was fully in! That was my pattern, I guess. Once I decided to go in a certain direction, I was committed. This was true in seeking the meaning of life, setting off to surf and live in Hawaii, in marriage, in my employment and in all I did.

For the next three years I poured my life into seeking God, reading his Word, attending fellowship four services a week, and was fully committed to serving Him. I was asked if I would go to the Philippines as a missionary. I think because of my self-confidence learned in growing up I said yes with no hesitation. I was going there alone, with no companions, and was excited to go. It was a real adventure for me. I stayed on the island of Mindanao, which had a lot of very remote areas. In fact, just about that same time they discovered an indigenous sort of pre-historic group of people living in a very remote part of the island. I think their discovery was published in the National Geographic magazine. At that time there were intermittent rebel kidnappings and killings. A couple of years after I returned home, the pastor I worked with sent me a very troubling picture that clearly told of the violence and darkness of the rebel issue. One of the rebels had come to church and accepted Jesus as his Savior. He brought with him a jar full of preserved human ears from the people he had killed. Something I was ignorant of when I went there. It was a rough neighborhood in spots, for sure.

When I landed on Mindanao on a flight from Manilla, I remember thinking I was being plunked down in the middle of a jungle. There was no airport terminal anywhere. It was more like a carport roof area surrounded by lush tropical vegetation with my greeters standing by the runway. I lived in a stilt home, build over a tidal wash with palm leaf shingles for the roof. There was an open area between the top of the walls and the roof for air movement and easy access for flying pests. The mosquitos were so heavy at night that I would crouch by the bed, which was covered with mosquito netting, and as fast as I could, I would lift it and jump into the bed. The next twenty minutes was spent trying to kill the little winged blood suckers who had gotten in with me. And I could never get them all! Allowing some of them to stay there was the price of getting to sleep.

It was so hot they said you could fry an egg on the sidewalk in Surigao Del Norte, near where I stayed. It sure felt that way to me! For the first few weeks I felt like a fried egg.

The "shower" was a fifty-gallon metal barrel, and a dipper to get the water onto your body. For a toilet, there was a real one, but no plumbing under it. Your contribution to the "sewer system" would fall beneath the stilt home, which was maybe fifteen feet above the tidal area. The movement of the ocean tides from high to low was the "flush" for the toilet. That worked okay until a rich local Chinese man built a road to his property which blocked most of the tidal flow. And there was no plunger big enough to fix that mess. It sure made me appreciate our life in America! I left shortly after that and never did hear how the sewer issue was resolved, if it ever was.

My trip to Mindanao ended when the Philippine president, Marcos, declared martial law. It was difficult to get up to Manilla for the plane flight home. One of the brothers in the church there was in the military and helped me set up the travel out of the country. I had to take an old ferry boat to another island. It was an overnight trip, so everyone had a cot. I remember putting my travel trunk under my cot. It was too tall, so I never slept that night as the trunk pushed up through the cot. But at least I knew where it was, and my things were safe. I didn't trust leaving it where someone could get into it if I slept. Some people there loved

Americans, others did not, so I was always on guard. From there I took a small plane to Manilla, with a crate of chickens sitting behind me, and then finally home. My trip to the Philippines was a life changing experience, and one that taught me how lucky we are to live in America.

I did want to get married and have kids. One time in Hawaii, when I was out behind our shack on the side of Haleakala, in Omaopio near Kula, on Maui, I was playing my Martin guitar and worshipping alone. I would frequently go out at night down a little ravine to sing and worship with my guitar. This one night I was having a real blessed communion with the Lord. I asked God for children. As clear as anyone's human voice would sound, God said to me, "You will have many children." Well, I had two kids. The "many children" came at age sixty-six, when between my wife and I we have six kids and twelve grandkids. God knew that way back then. The path to getting there was interesting, and certainly not direct, but I did arrive in the promise He made to me that night. Thank you, Lord,

During my surfing years, I had many surfing trips up and down the coast. I always dreamed and yearned for a "surfer girl" to share my life. I cannot put it into words, but there was a deep yearning for a companion in life. It was very deep and strong. The perfect dream girl would ride in my VW van with me, sharing all of the fun surf and ocean adventures. I did not have a specific list of the attributes and qualities of such a dream girl, but there was an intense yearning to share my life with someone special. That dream came true at age sixty-six, when Deborah came into my life. My first marriage was a hope for a dream girl and a wishing for the fulfilling of my heart's yearning, but it never worked out nor materialized.

I got married the first time when I was twenty-three, to a girl from the Christian fellowship we were attending. I remember the minister telling me I was perhaps more in love with the idea of marriage than the girl. He was right. The first six months of the marriage were constant torment and stress. It was pure turmoil! She was an only child, had been stifled and controlled by her mother, and her mom was determined to not let her go. Her mom actually wanted us to move into a "to be built" apartment above their garage. But we planned to move to Hawaii. Her mother would call and have my ex in a state of severe emotional distress time and time again. My ex could not process her way out of the turmoil. Over a few days the episode would subside, only to rise and repeat itself again frequently. I was really damaged by all of this but hung in thinking I must. There was a physical reaction in my gut every time the phone rang, wondering if it was her mother ready to attack once again. Looking back, I think God gave me six months with no pregnancy to get out of the marriage. I simply did not see it then. My frame of mind was that I was married, and I could not change that. Marriage was not escapable, and I was stuck! I should have taken her home to her parents and gone on my way …. alone. I must say here that I am greatly blessed with my daughter and my grandkids. I would not give them up for anything, so even a difficult marriage produced some really great blessings. This has not been so true with my son, which I will share later.

My life had gone from freedom, surfing, and finding God to being in a marriage that created much heart ache and confusion for me. Deborah had entered into a similar situation, but she didn't get to have the fun young adult experiences that I had. The following is the story of her marriage.

Chapter Six

Surfer Girl

DEBORAH'S YOUNG ADULTHOOD
PREGNANCY AND MARRIAGE

When I was seventeen, I decided I wanted to drink on a holiday weekend. I had never had alcohol except for a small glass of champagne at holiday dinners with my aunt. I was with a friend and my sister, Paula. We went to a parade on Halloween Day and then to a college party. I had toed the line until then. I met my future husband at the party. I was a senior in high school, and he was in college. We began to date, and I started drinking at parties and ended up pregnant. In 1969 pregnancy led to marriage, so I was married at the end of my senior year of high school. I had my son two weeks after my eighteenth birthday. My son was beautiful with dark hair, and I loved watching him develop and grow.

I was married for thirty-five years and had three more daughters. My ex became a doctor, and I went through the whole process of medical school, internship, and residency with him. The marriage was very difficult. He had an anger problem just like my mother, and he had a drinking problem. I suffered emotional and psychological attacks from him. I continued the behavior patterns

I had learned growing up; to put myself and feelings aside to calm him down. And if I tried to speak up, he would shut me down easily just as my father and mother had done.

I have suppressed many of my memories and even of years of my marriage. It was so painful. When we were first married, I found that my ex had a short fuse. We would go to basketball games, and he would scream loudly the whole game. Someone asked me if that embarrassed me. Yes, it did. But he wouldn't stop, even if I asked him. This behavior continued throughout the marriage. He would yell at football games – and he had a loud voice. Later, he would yell and scream at the kid's soccer and softball games. One time he got kicked out of the entire baseball field from yelling at one of the kid's games. But this didn't deter him. He didn't care if it embarrassed me or the kids or if people told him to be quiet

He used threats skillfully. From the very beginning of the marriage, he would threaten to leave if he didn't like what was being said or done, or if I had displeased him. Many times, after he had thrown a fit in public about something, he would take off and leave me stranded with a child or two and no way of getting home. Once, He left my son and me at my sister's college dorm, embarrassing me in front of my sister and her friends. He would yell, use physically aggressive body language, and storm out. Another time, he got mad while playing a touch football game with his friends and threw a fit, yelled that they were being unfair, and left because he wasn't playing well. I was so humiliated. He also had road rage. I was often terrified as he accelerated at other drivers, honked the horn, and yelled as he weaved in and out of traffic using the car as a weapon.

I was very young, had a baby and we were at poverty level. I was trapped. I knew my parents would not support me if I left the marriage. I was on my own and had to be very responsible.

The marriage was good at times and bad at times – just like my growing up years. It was familiar. The abuse cycle that I had experienced growing up continued. It contained verbal and psychological abuse from my ex (I would get really quiet or try to calm him down), a honeymoon period (where I acted as if nothing had happened), a period of calm and then a tension building period or episode leading to him exploding at me. I learned to repress my feelings and emotions and to even deny them. I was very good at calming my ex down when he was raging or berating me emotionally. When a person is verbally abused continually, those damaging words get into the brain and heart. It is almost better to be hit physically because then you know you have been hit. Verbal and psychological abuse leaves unseen scars that can be very deep. Evans, The Verbally Abusive Relationship.

In the meantime, Kirk married at age twenty-three and also was very challenged in his marriage. Here is more of his story.

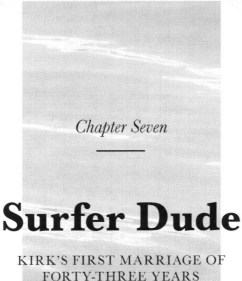

Chapter Seven

Surfer Dude

KIRK'S FIRST MARRIAGE OF
FORTY-THREE YEARS

Looking back, I can see the mental illness that plagued my ex-wife's mother, and in some ways in my wife also, and this was certainly part of the problem I married into. My ex-father-in-law had been a music producer in Nashville. Her mother was supposedly a Christian, as was her father. Soon after our marriage, her mother thought that she and her husband were under threat of harm and retaliation from some group opposed to their particular ministry. I am not even sure what ministry this could have been. This was totally fabricated and crazy with no basis in fact. Her mother had mental issues. She convinced her husband to quit his successful career and sell their home as they needed to live "underground" to be safe. They became house sitters for Christians who were on vacation. They lived the rest of their lives with no home base. It was very sad to watch. There are always fringe elements of Christianity which use the Bible to justify some pretty strange behavior.

When my ex-father-in-law was dying they were living in a

hotel. Someone was paying for their room, and their dinner was the nightly appetizers served to the hotel guests. My ex-mother-in-law would tell us how good the food was. Really? His heart was failing, but her mother would not call a doctor. She said faith would heal him or he would die. He died in the hotel room; a doctor never being called. She made it sound so wonderful. I felt sick!

For the first seven years of my marriage, my wife's mother would call and rage on the phone at either my ex or me. There was also spiritual darkness in her mother. I could sense the demonic forces. I knew them very well. I could feel their evil presence when she was on the attack. There was always this cloud of demonic presence I could sense, which was manipulative, accusatory, demeaning and hateful if not yielded to. When she was dying years later, I was in the room when she passed away. Those demonic spirits left her body, and I felt them again as they left her. They were very familiar. They then exited the room through the window. I do not know their names, but I knew their presence very well from years of them attacking me through my ex's mom. I will never forget it. That was God showing me that the attacks I had endured for so many years were at least partly because of spiritual darkness.

At one point, out of the blue after many years of being attacked and tormented, followed by a few more years of total disconnect when we heard nothing from her, we received a phone call from my ex's mom. She had previously cut us off for a few years, declaring that we were not her daughter nor son-in-law and that she had no interest at all in the grandchildren. But, on this day she had decided it was the year of Jubilee and we could connect again. I was reluctant to do this but felt some sense of obligation to allow the in-laws to meet the grandkids. I don't know why, but that is how I felt. They really did not deserve to meet them, had never apologized for their abuse toward us, but we met with them as requested. We met for an hour in a hotel room where they were staying, and they met the grandchildren. It was awkward to say the least. Demented? I think so! I share some of this so you can get a bit of the backdrop that set the stage for a very difficult marriage.

And my ex had issues of her own. I think partly from genetics, partly from how she was raised, and from what else I'm not sure. Anyway, I became "codependent in chief" for her weaknesses and stood in the gap between her and her mom mostly, and her dad sometimes. At times I was the "codependent in chief" taking over responsibilities I should have left with her, and at other times I was "enabler in chief" putting up with and allowing some crazy behavior. I made excuses in my own heart and mind for my ex, rather than seeing things for what they were. Years later, I became too exhausted with it all to try anymore.

Every time her mother would call her, my ex would be a basket case for hours and days. I had to fix everything, or so I thought and wrongly accepted a role no other person should ever take on. Each person must find a way to recover themselves from their own problems and bondages. II Timothy 2:26 says it pretty well; "… and they may come to their senses and escape from the snare of the devil…" (English Standard Version). I finally learned that I could not change one thing in my ex, or in anyone else. It is what it is. And I would have been wiser to accept the reality of what I saw, heard and experienced. It was very clear. I didn't see this though, until forty plus years later.

I felt trapped! In my religious thinking mind, I had made a lifelong commitment and could never leave. This personal torment was mine until death. I never entertained a divorce in the early years. We even went to marriage seminars, became a sharing couple, all the while I was feeling like I was moving to be more and more alone in the marriage. It takes two folks working on their relationship to make it work. After a marriage seminar weekend there would be a brief span of things being better, but then the same old stuff would resurface. I worked at employing the skills I had learned about marriage and the role of the husband. But I felt often as if I was pouring out all my effort on the floor. I felt hopeless and trapped but put up a good front while not being honest with myself.

We had two children, a boy and a girl. I poured myself into supporting them, changed jobs to be at home more and took a pay cut to put the family first. That in itself was a good decision, but it only served to delay addressing my marital problems. Even from a very difficult marriage, two wonderful kids were born. That part I do not regret at all, as they were a special blessing to me.

The stress of our relationship, following the first six months of heavy torment, was seven more years of extreme up and downs with my ex's mother. That never really did heal and was a torment at times until the day of my ex-mother-in-law's death many years later. There was always intermittent turmoil. I became accustomed to turmoil and abuse, from my mother-in-law directly, and from the trauma she caused in my ex-wife which always overflowed to me. I guess I thought it was normal, or at least I told myself that was the case. I had no idea of what a healthy marriage was like. But now I do, with Deborah!

My ex was very deficient in being able to handle some of the normal stresses of life. During the day when I was at work, (no cell phones then), things would happen with her parents; perhaps a call, or with one of the kids at home or at school, and she could not navigate through the issue, whatever it was. It became common for her to store up her anger, rage or have a histrionic reaction to the event, saving it for me when I got home. The moment I would walk in the front door from work, she would unload on me to fix whatever it was. Always with great emotional discharge, volcanic in force which was frankly at times overwhelming. There was never a, "Hi, honey how was your day." I can't remember one! I was dog tired from a very long day in the office, and then came the burden of fixing her distresses. Normally over not very much at all, but to her it seemed the end of the world. The tempest of her reactions was exhausting, and all too common.

It got to where I hated to go home. I hated opening the front door because I knew that too many times problems, greatly blown out of proportion, awaited me. I would pause in my car in the driveway and wonder what would hit me when I went inside. I can still physically feel my stomach tightening and the internal upset that I experienced as I write about it yet today. A call at work or hearing her voice caused the same reaction. Which I would experience when she went "over the edge" on some small issue. I was in the trap of enduring for the sake of the kids and because of my religious thinking. Both were a prison sentence for me. But the day was coming when I would break out of jail!

I think I was suffering from the very real trauma because of this stuff. Probably some level of Post-Traumatic Stress Disorder from the constant upheaval. On some occasions she would call me at work and demand that I come home immediately as there was a crisis. I would talk her into a state of some calmness, and deal with it later. I cannot recall one issue that was of any magnitude to require my going home. It was always about her emotional raging or distress set off by some normal life or child experience. She was greatly incapacitated too many times when it came to handling the things of normal life.

As the kids grew older and started sprouting their wings of independence, she would frequently get into a rage toward one of them about some normal developmental issue or rebellious streak. She seemed to light into our son more than our daughter. And our daughter seemed to weather the storms better than our son. On many occasions I would physically stand between them and demand that their mother stop her raging. I would demand that we talk in our room and would send the kids to their rooms. That was the only way to stop the raging. This behavior I learned when my parents would fight when drinking too much and I would get between them to stop the fighting.

Her rages always became personal attacks. She would tell the kids, "You're stupid!" To a young child, such proclamations are damaging and affect their self-image. The kids were being damaged! I would patch it up as best I could, apologize for their mom's words, and keep going. Interesting, that I never recall my ex ever saying she was sorry about any of the rages. It was always someone else's fault, and she was justified in her behavior. I cannot remember her ever apologizing to the kids for her screaming at them. On the other hand, when I made parenting mistakes, I would always go and apologize to the child when I saw I had been in error. On a couple of occasions, I was so aggravated and pumped up from the rages of my ex toward the kids that I would spank them too hard, or yell at them too much. The tsunami of emotions erupting from her would overflow onto and into me, and I would react. My reactions were wrong, I know that, but that is how it worked. One time my son was screaming at me belligerently, and I spit in his face. On a different occasion, when he was screaming at me, I slapped his face. I am ashamed of those two occurrences, although the way he was speaking to me the one time, the spit in the face was probably warranted, but I should not have done it. The slap was very wrong. In both cases, I felt terrible and apologized profusely. Years later, my son's wife said that I was always his hero. So, I guess I did enough good in raising them that the few occurrences of my errors did not do too much damage. At least I pray so.

Things were not very good at home, with the tensions of child rearing and my ex's parents interjecting their venom into our existence. One time when I was on a business trip, I called home to talk to my ex and the kids. There was no answer. There were no cell phones then. I called back later, well past the kid's bedtime, and there was still no answer. On the third call, late at night, she answered. She had been to dinner with an engaged single man from our church, an elder actually, at his fiancées home, with the kids. The fiancée was not home as she was working. This guy had previously confided in me that he had problems with his sexual appetite for women, and many of his encounters were with married women. You can imagine how I felt when she told me where she had been. She had to tell me because the kids would have let me know. She denied that anything went on, but I will never know for sure. I felt heart sick. On that business trip one of the female salespeople tried to get me to go with her into her room. I was not interested. After several refusals to do so, she ended up leaving the after-work party with another man. She was determined to go to bed with someone that night. So here I am being "Mr. Noble", and my ex is out to dinner with a guy with a sex addiction.

After about twenty-five to thirty years of marriage my ex became paranoid. She was convinced that jet trails in the sky were a plot by the government to poison us poor souls down on earth. She insisted I listen to radio shows about this evil plot. I did once, just to see how bizarre it all really was. She also hoarded out of fear. If she needed a transistor radio, she would purchase six of them. If she needed lightbulbs, she would ask me to purchase many of them. I, as codependent as I was, enabled this ridiculous behavior just to stop the out-of-control rants of fear. I had given up trying. I had actually been living a separate life in the same house and enabled her out of order behavior for the sake of quiet in the home. She had stated she did not want any sexual relations, she had "done that enough in our marriage," which led to living separate lives, in separate bedrooms in the same house. If I attempted to discuss not buying so much stuff, or that I felt much of her thinking was non-realistic conspiracy thinking, I was the stupid one, the ignorant one, the problem. I would suffer the verbal abuse for my differing opinion with personal attacks and belittling. Remember, I thought I had to stay in the marriage until death, and quietness from her was worth buying some lightbulbs if it meant peace. I recall trying to help her reign in her hoarding and buying. One year, she spent around $100,000 on shopping from the television. And this was for stuff that was not really needed. She would buy four of some items "because they might not have it again". When I finally got divorced, the garage and closets were so full of hoarded stuff it took several truckloads of help from Got Junk to clean it all out. She would not listen to reason. Fearful, mentally challenged minds don't receive sound reason very well.

I spent as much time as possible downstairs in our house, away from her. Or I would stay at my business office, which was about twenty minutes from the house, even though I didn't need to be there. At least it was a safe quiet place with no ridicule.

Because I was downstairs a lot, she even demanded that I put in a doorbell, so she could ring it from upstairs. I would hear it when I was downstairs and could come back upstairs to her beck and call. I am so disappointed in myself that I allowed all of this crazy stuff. I feel really stupid! But I was in a mental prison and at that point the prison doors were not yet open.

Over the years, I would excuse her behavior, and her always blaming me. But now I recall many times when the Lord would whisper in my heart, "She has a problem, it is not you, it is really her". I ignored this so many times I cannot count them. I saw the issues, but my mental processing was greatly flawed, both with my ex and with her parents, as it was filtered through the framework of thinking which said, "you must stay married no matter what". Therefore, the clarity of the reality I was living in was muddled. Thus, I dismissed the truth and walked forward rejecting the reality. Later I came to accept the facts for what they were and that helped set me free. I was upset with myself, felt very stupid, as all of the mess of the past made sense now. I was not the problem, and I had accepted that she had issues, very real ones! I learned that it is wise to see things as they are, and not excuse them. It could have saved me from a great deal of anguish if I had accepted things as they were and not as I hoped they were. I wish I had lived with my eyes open!

During these years I kept some level of sanity by developing other activates. I took up pistol, rifle and shotgun shooting and some competition events such as skeet shooting, sporting clays, and martial arts. I would take long hikes or bike rides into the mountains and spend time with God. I worked out regularly, swam, ran, biked and exercised which also helped my mental stability. Later I got back into surfing also - the sport I truly love!

I would also spend time regularly worshipping God with my guitar. My ex would say I was "howling at the moon". She was good at demeaning me and launching personal attacks. She was supposedly a Christian, but when I would worship downstairs in our home, this is what she would say to me. She expressed no interest at all in worshipping with me, never!

Then grandkids came along, four of them. Wonderful kids! My son got a divorce when his kids were young. Things were very ugly between him and his wife, and we ended up raising his two children a majority of the time over the next eleven years. They were a joy for me, and I cherish the time I had with them! I would not exchange that for anything. But raising them also delayed my addressing my own marital problems. I put the grandkids first. During the divorce, we actually had to help my daughter-in law rather than our son for the best interests of the grandkids. Because of this, my relationship with my son became a casualty during his divorce. He behaved just like my ex-mother-in-law and like my ex-wife with personal attacks, hatred and extreme vitriol. I had interjected myself into the divorce for the benefit of the grandkids. Had I not done so; things may not have gotten quite so bad. Looking back, I might have handled it differently, with not so much direct involvement. To this day my son remains estranged from a relationship with me. There had been brief times of reconnecting, but they never lasted. A sorrowful part of my life. We have a great relationship with my daughter, her husband and two kids, a boy and a girl.

At one point when I was focused on getting the family back together and healed from the traumas of my son's divorce I reached out to my son. I ended up apologizing for things I had not done wrong and moving off of my positions on some things that had occurred, even though I was in the right, just to try and patch things up. I was acting as the peace maker, the "fixer" of things again. The problem was that there was no heart attitude change on his part. So, my efforts ended up failing, as all of the bitterness in him came back out again and again in one form or another. I should have left it all alone until he came to want a relationship and could apologize for what he did wrong. He never did apologize and there was no real change in his heart, so reentering into a relationship with him was doomed to fail. I should have been smarter and held the boundaries I had in place. I forgave him for the sake of my own heart so as not to become bitter and resentful. But that did not mean I could have a relationship with him - not until his own heart had changed. It was not my role to fix or help him, but to stand in my boundaries until he had a change of heart.

Sort of like the story of the prodigal son. The father did not run to his son until his son had a change of heart. That needed to occur first as until that were to happen, my concessions meant nothing. Had the father sought to seek the prodigal son too early, his son would have resented him even more.

Philippians 1:9 says that our love should be with "knowledge and all discernment". (English Standard Version). Love that is without discernment and knowledge is like uncontrolled water flowing all over the place and causing damage. This is similar to when flood waters wash away the rich topsoil in a field. Love with knowledge and discernment channels the water where it needs to be and is productive, causing no damage. It is like water flowing through irrigation ditches and lines into the field as needed, not overflowing, or damaging the soil. Doing good and showing "love" errantly can actually be very damaging. There are times when withholding assistance and love is the appropriate conduct, similar to the father of the prodigal son. He withheld all of his blessing and love for his son until the right time.

I think part of my son's issue was definitely from the treatment he received from his mother. It is complicated for sure, and much more to it than that alone, but I am convinced it contributed to the problems. Had I not been so involved with his divorce, and co-raising the grandkids for the following eleven years, I believe I would have dealt with my own marriage issues sooner. Hindsight is 20/20, as they say. I regret deeply not dealing with my own failed marriage much earlier.

My ex-wife's behavior she had exhibited with our children, repeated itself with the grandkids, who would spend up to five days a week with us. She was always questioning them about their mother, or their dad, and what was going on. This was to the point of harassment and was certainly out of line. She would not stop until I stepped between them. I found myself in the same role as before; peacemaker and "fixer" stepping in-between the argument. It was during this time that I began to allow myself to think that I was not the cause of all the conflicts and that my ex really had issues. The constant cloud affecting my thinking, due to all too frequent personal attacks and belittling, began to lift and I began to see things as there truly were. This started freeing me from my mental prison. I began to see how I was being disobedient to what God was trying to tell me. I had refused to acknowledge the reality of my ex-wife's conduct and the depth of her problems and as a result kids and grandkids had been and were being damaged. Disobedience carries consequences for many surrounding us. In my case, me, my children and my grandchildren. I should have taken action forty years sooner! I was bound in wrong thinking which blinded me. I was not being honest with myself and had given up on trying to change things.

My business career was always good. My work ethic was strong and paid off. I started in the wholesale distribution business as a warehouse stocker and forklift operator. From there I was promoted through a series of opportunities to Vice President of a smaller private company with operations in Florida, Mexico, the Caribbean, Missouri, and Texas. It was from this position I changed jobs to be at home more. I was travelling too many days per month, was absent for my kid's activities and decided to make a change to be a father who could be more involved with their lives. I had missed my dad's time with me as a kid and wanted to do better than that for my children. I took a substantial pay cut in the process of this change, but God was always faithful to provide. A year later He began to financially bless me, and that continued for many years.

But before that happened, I had accepted a job in Washington state and moved the family there. This was a job that would have had no travel and would have allowed for more time with the family. The first day on the job after we had just hung the last picture on the wall of our new home, I was called into the office and told that my position had been eliminated! Well, we arranged for our things to be put in storage and stayed with friends for about three to four months. This was stressful but refreshing in a way. The kids thought it was a great adventure! They walked through the countryside to a small schoolhouse, where our friends taught school. They got along great with our friends' two kids, and still to this day speak about what fun it was for them. Then the Lord opened the door to return us to an area near our former home and near the lake, where we purchased and operated a small wholesale supply store. I think God was keeping me in the area for the destiny of meeting my second wife, Deborah!

About one year later, a company I had consulted with while working for my former employer, was looking for me to manage one of their warehouse locations that I had helped them get going during my consulting year for them. The job was to be a six-month assignment with no promise of anything past that as they were planning to sell the company. I initially said no, because we were doing ok financially, and I had a lot of time with my kids. I was coaching softball and soccer and being with them a great deal of the time. At one point I built a full-size volleyball court in our back yard for my son because he played on the high school team.

A few months later, the company called me again, and this time I met with them and accepted the six-month assignment. Well, the sale never happened. Six months turned into thirty-five years! A few years into the thirty-five, when I was driving home from work, the Lord said to me as clear as a bell, "I am going to give you something of your own." I had no idea what that meant and was puzzled. The next day my boss called me in and ask me if I wanted to purchase the company with him. I said "Yes, but I do not have any money. How are we going to do that?" It turned out that the owners wanted out quickly. Remember they originally hired me with the plan to sell in six months. So, we were able to buy it for the next five years with sweat equity. This meant that we would give them all the profits for the next five years. The deal was done, and thirty- five years later, we were still running that company. More on that later.

Now let us return to the story of my divorce after forty-three years of marriage. I admit, I am a slow learner! After my divorce, my ex found others to enable her. She was particularly good at that. When I vacated the role of enabler, others arrived to take my place. She became enamored with a young single man in his late twenties, (she was in her sixties), from her new church who was helping her with household matters and errands. She bought a very expensive motorcycle for him, keeping it in her garage, upon which she fantasized she would ride with him. She hoped to marry him, but his parents said no, they wanted grandkids. She funded his music production, so much so that the banker in charge of her financial affairs called me to ask if there was anything I could do, as tens of thousands of dollars were being given to this young man, including the promise of the deed to her home upon her death. I share this to give some insight into what I left, and perhaps a little of the why.

There are always two sides to a story like mine. I am not saying I was perfect. I was not. I became angry and mean at times and so frustrated that it seemed the only way I could get my point across was to raise my voice. I should have simply accepted what things really were and changed my path. But I had chains on my feet, I couldn't leave. Chains of wrong religious thinking, and a chained person lashes out sometimes. I was wrong to do this and ashamed I did. There were good times too. And my ex was a very nurturing mother when the kids were younger.

We had the stresses of my ex's parents when the kids were

younger, and then the emotional outbreaks as the kids grew up and became more independent. It finally became clear to me that my marriage was not good for me or my ex. It was unhealthy and damaging. We brought out the worst in each other too much of the time. I would raise my voice to stop the insanity too many times. Early in the marriage, I was so frustrated in her not being able to come down from an emotional crisis about her mother, that I threw my new leather-bound Bible across the room to the floor. I loved that Bible; it was my favorite Thompson Chain reference version. I felt like I had thrown it into the face of God. I felt sick. On many nights for the first years of our marriage I would spend hours, until one or two in the morning talking with my ex, attempting to bring her out of an emotional, hysterical outbreak. I should have taken her home to her parents and annulled the marriage! But I didn't, as I thought it was for me to fix this and endure it as my cross to bear. My codependent conduct was very severe and crippling my ex and destroying me. I was assuming the role of fixing all of her issues, which only she could fix. I took them upon myself mentally and emotionally and for that I paid a heavy price of internal stresses that were not mine. I was dying inside because of the constant emotional storm I lived in. In nature the storms always pass, even the worst. But for me, the storm continued, almost daily for years…. for years!

The blessing of my kids and grandkids did make the marriage worth it in that regard. I do not regret having them!

For the last twelve years of my marriage, I felt like the heavens were brass. God seemed to not be listening to me. I never stopped praying or worshipping, but the relationship with Him was cold. That is because for years He wanted me to be honest with myself and face my situation. It was something I avoided, made excuses for and failed to address. Any form of disobedience will dull our interaction with God until corrected. I was being disobedient, and I see that now. I wish I had seen it sooner.

My ex had decided, seven years prior to our divorce, that she was done with any sexual relationship. She had "had enough sex in the past years" and didn't need or want it anymore. She said my hands were too rough, like sandpaper (Deborah loves my touch and my hands). She said I snored and kept her awake every night, so we slept in separate bedrooms. I had heard so much complaining that I finally said, I will sleep in another room. With very little sex it really didn't matter anyway. (Deborah says I rarely snore). On the few occasions when we did have sex, she would say, "Can't you hurry up and be done." After that comment, it was all over for me. That made me feel sick. And during our marriage, she would often make comments that made me feel that normal sexual relations were dirty. God created our sexuality! To Him, it is a beautiful thing to be fully enjoyed in marriage and is a very important part of marriage. Why didn't I accept things for what they were? I was blinded by my religious thinking, and a captive imprisoned by it. I thought God would disown me if I divorced. I felt I would greatly disappoint Him if I left my marriage. Later, it was He who ran to me as the father to the prodigal son, embracing me, comforting me and blessing me as the welcomed home wayward son. His grace and mercy, and compassion are fathomless!

The point being is that my ex-wife was making excuses for not wanting a sexual relationship. I truly believe that the only real reason she had sex was to have kids. Once that was accomplished, her interest waned. There were some early signs of frigidity, even on our honeymoon. She didn't want me to see her naked in the bathtub. I never understood that. It seemed like to her sex was to have kids and not for pure pleasure. Over the years she was only too happy to have our intimacy occur less frequently, until she declared it was over. And if I did want to have sex, she would often call me a "pervert" for wanting to make love, making me feel guilty for a very normal and blessed desire, which God created. And I am not talking about any weird or kinky sex. These were clear signals that there was something very wrong and it wasn't the roughness of the skin on my hands.

And I would also eat dinner alone, downstairs. I recall the peace I would feel when I finally finished cooking dinner upstairs and could take it downstairs and sit and watch the news or some show. It was comforting to be there, away from her, and enjoying a meal by myself. Funny how that is a pleasant memory for me now, and sad that I got myself into that bad of a situation and ignored the reality. We were separated, living under the same roof, but our relationship was over. But I was still stuck to a large degree in my mind, not yet accepting that a divorce was for sure the right way out for me. We were only married on paper.

Toward the end of our marriage, my ex said she did not want to cook, and she complained about my cooking, so I arranged for a personal chef to come to the house once a week and cook several days' worth of food. I was willing to do way too much to stop the complaining and have peace in my prison.

Throughout my forty-three years of marriage, I had refused to accept and see things as they really were. My mind was so stilted with unhealthy religious thinking. I made excuses for my ex's behavior and refused to admit that at times it was really off base. That was probably partly because that would mean I made a mistake and chose the wrong girl. That would be embarrassing to me. Ego and pride are always a danger. And by excusing her behavior I could stay in the marriage, because of my stilted thinking and errant understanding of God and divorce. I cannot tell you how liberating it was to finally accept and admit that things were really what they were. I endured lifelong friendships being broken off because of some rather insignificant thing one of them had said or done that would cause my ex to cut them off. I put my marriage first in an inordinate way, and I paid the price. After my divorce, at least three of my friends and family said, "We saw it all along." They KNEW what was wrong. I did not allow myself to see it! Lord, forgive me!

For many years, when it got too bad, I entertained the thought of suicide. I knew how I would do it, and I had a location in mind as well. Even though I would think about it, I knew I could never actually do it, because of a conscience toward God. I feared taking my own life, but the thought of doing so was to me, at the time, a last-ditch option, sort of. Knowing I couldn't do it conflicted with using it as an option. It was strange, but it gave some form of pressure release to think about getting out, even if through suicide, because it was at least an escape. The terrible thing is that I never stopped and said to myself, "Listen, you're thinking of taking your life because of how things are in your marriage. Wake up and realize that something is really wrong here. Look at getting out!" I never did that, even though it should have been a huge warning sign to me. That is how captive I was to my religious thinking, which was crushing me and suffocating my life. I could not pray to God about a divorce. I could not mention that word to Him in prayer, but I could entertain taking my life to get out! Think about that! When I did finally pray to Him about divorce, He ran to meet me! He was my prodigal Father, running to help me when I turned to Him!

My grandson, when he was little, got physically stuck in a chair. He cried out, "Hep me, I'm guck." He was stuck. So was I! But it took years for me to cry out to God, "Help me, I'm stuck!"

Over the years, I fellowshipped in several different churches. I wanted to be a "doer of good works" for God. Our self-ego seeks to do stuff for God, when what He wants is our heart and for us to understand that it is His grace that saves and helps us, not our works. The law leads to death, but faith and grace lead to life. I served as Associate Pastor, led Bible studies, led worship, and had home Bible studies. I took all of this very seriously. For over twenty-five years I wrote a monthly letter sharing a brief scriptural message with a few hundred persons mailing list. I later compiled these into four books.

I had a few very painful experiences with Church. On one occasion, in a fellowship where I would help lead worship, give Bible studies, and rotate as leader for study groups, I was asked by the Pastor to present a teaching on the Baptism of the Holy Spirit. This fellowship did believe in the Baptism of the Holy Spirit and the operation of the gifts of the Spirit, but things did not work out too well. The night of the teaching the fellowship was pretty full, maybe forty people. For the small church that was about 80% full. I gave the lesson and asked if anyone wanted to receive the Holy Spirit baptism. About fourteen people lined up to be prayed with. The Holy Spirit met them one by one as they were prayed for, and they each prayed in the spirit (tongues) and glorified God. It was a very special time and was decent and in order. The one person who did not receive the prayer language had said to me, "If what you say is correct, I would like the Baptism of the Holy Spirit." The problem there was the "if." God had not yet made it real or clear to this person. You either believe it and receive it, or you don't. Unbelief and doubt hinder the moving of the Holy Spirit.

Anyway, the next day the Pastor, who had been there in the lobby during the whole evening before (interesting that he never came into the meeting room), and had seen how many people responded called me into his office. He basically said, "We can't walk together in ministry, so you will need to leave the church." After asking me to teach on the subject, and after witnessing the

Holy Spirit bear witness with the message with so many people responding for the baptism of the Spirit he told me to leave. Why did he ask me to teach on the subject? Why didn't he come into the meeting himself? Only God knows what the motives were. Jesus never kicks us out of His church, but as far as earthly fellowships, well that is a different story.

At this point, let me share a little about the Baptism of the Holy Spirit.

Ask yourself this question, "What importance did the Church fathers place upon the Baptism of the Holy Spirit?" And "What importance did Jesus place upon the Baptism of the Holy Spirit?"

What did Jesus instruct his disciples after He rose from the dead? And think on this for one moment; were they born again and saved at this point? They had learned of Him during His ministry with them. They knew He was the Messiah. They had seen Him die. They had seen Him Resurrected. Thomas cried out, "My Lord and my God." Jesus was seen by them forty days after His resurrection, sharing with them the things of the kingdom of God. I believe they were certainly born again when Jesus said the following things to them.

In Mark 16:15-18, Jesus says to them, "Go into all the world and proclaim the gospel to the whole creation. Whoever believes and is baptized will be saved, but whoever does not believe will be condemned. And these signs will accompany those who believe in my name they will cast out demons: they will speak in new tongues; they will pick up serpents with their hands; and if they drink any deadly poison, it will not hurt them; they will lay their hands on the sick, and they will recover." (English Standard Version)

Acts: 1:3-8 selected passages: "... to whom also he shewed himself alive after his passion by many infallible proofs, being seen of them forty days, and speaking of the things pertaining to the kingdom of God: and being assembled together with them, commanded them that they should not depart from Jerusalem, but wait for the promise of the Father, which saith he, ye have heard of me. For John truly baptized with water; but you shall be baptized with the Holy Ghost not many days hence....ye shall receive power, after that the Holy Ghost is come upon you; and ye shall be witnesses unto me...unto the uttermost part of the earth." (King James Version)

Jesus had commanded them to go into all the world and preach the Gospel to every creature, but here He clarifies, "but not just yet". You first need to be baptized with the Holy Spirit. They needed the power of the Holy Spirit. They needed the gifting of the Holy Spirit. Jesus commanded them to wait for it. It was not a request, but a command.

Did the apostles carry this priority, being baptized by the Holy Spirit, into their ministry after Jesus ascended into heaven? In Acts 2, the disciples received the baptism of the Holy Spirit themselves, and Jesus words were fulfilled. They received the Holy Spirit as He said they would, and they also spoke with other tongues as the Spirit gave them utterance, as Jesus had said.

In Acts 8, Phillip was evangelizing in Samaria, and people were saved, devils were being cast out, and healings were occurring. Again, a fulfillment of Jesus' words. When the disciples heard about this, they immediately sent Peter and John "who...prayed for them that they might receive the Holy Ghost." Acts 8:15, (KJV) Basically they said, "Alright guys, there are a bunch of new believers over there in Samaria. Peter and John, you go over there and make sure they receive the Holy Spirit." For that is the first thing we read they did upon arriving there.

In Acts 10:44-46 we read of the first record of Gentiles receiving salvation and the baptism of the Holy Spirit. Peter is sharing with them the story of Jesus, his death and resurrection, and the remission of sins through believing in Him when the following occurred: "While Peter was still saying these things, the Holy Spirit fell on all who heard the word. And the believers from among the circumcised who had come with Peter were amazed because they were hearing them speaking in tongues and extolling God." (ESV) Here, the Holy Spirit Himself poured out, bearing witness with the words of Peter, and fulfilling the words of Jesus.

In Acts 19, Paul carried the importance of the Holy Spirit baptism in his work as well. As we read in verses 2-6 selected sections, "…and he said unto them, have ye received the Holy Ghost since ye believed? ….. and when Paul had laid his hands upon them, the Holy Spirit came on them; and they spoke with tongues and prophesied." (KJV)

The manifestations of the Holy Spirit, and His gifts intended to operate in and through the believer, are important basics to the faith. In Corinthians, Paul addresses this subject in detail. He criticized the out of order use of the gifts, while encouraging them when done decently and in order. He addresses the personal edification one receives from praying in the spirit (in tongues) in I Corinthians 14:4 saying, "he that speaks in an unknown tongue edifies himself." (KJV))

From a personal growth and edification point of view, Paul further explains in I Corinthians 14:14-19 selected passages: "if I pray in an unknown tongue, my spirit prays, but my understanding is unfruitful. What is it then? I will pray with the spirit, and I will pray with the understanding also: I will sing with the spirit, and I will sing with the understanding also…. I thank my God, I speak with tongues more than ye all: yet in the church I had rather speak five words with my understanding, that by my voice I might teach others also, than ten thousand words in an unknown tongue." (KJV)

My personal observation of Paul boasting that he spoke in

tongues more than everyone else is this: it would be rather haughty for him to say this if the prayer language of the Spirit was only for some believers and not available for all. I think that the prayer language of the spirit, to pray in tongues, is something available to every believer as a blessing in prayer and for edification. This statement is in no way a judgement upon those who do not use this prayer gift, nor a mandate that they must. It is an encouragement that it is available to all who ask and believe and that you can ask for it.

Now, back to our story and another not-so-great church experience.

In another fellowship, I was Associate Pastor sharing messages, Bible studies and worship. I was happy to help and be of service. Folks enjoyed my teaching and singing. Things were going well. Then the church hired a "professional" who was in the business of helping churches increase their numbers and mostly their tithe income. As Associate pastor I attended the seminars on how to accomplish getting more money coming from the flock. I was grieved! It was so different than what I felt was the way of the Spirit. Prior to the seminars God gave me a dream one night. I saw the pastor on stage presenting the message and all of a sudden, the wall behind him opened to reveal a commercial business operation behind the scenes of what appeared to be a church. When I attended the increasing money seminars, it all made sense. This church was not about feeding the flock, but about how to get more money from the flock. Long story short, one of the elders, the brother of the pastor was later arrested for mishandling money for a Christian music group. I left this fellowship of my own accord.

I never left Jesus, but I did leave the church. Over the years I have fellowshipped in many different churches. Those that lift Him up have more of the presence of the Holy Spirit in their gatherings. Those that follow professional programs and patterns seem to be on the dry side spiritually.

I always searched for God's direction and wanted to please Him. He kept His hand on me through those difficult years. Deborah had a different story with her first marriage, but God also kept her under his care during those years.

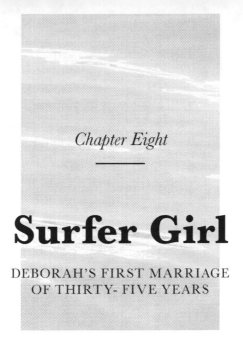

Chapter Eight

Surfer Girl

DEBORAH'S FIRST MARRIAGE
OF THIRTY- FIVE YEARS

We were very poor the first twelve years of our marriage. My ex was an undergraduate college student when we got married and wanted to be a medical doctor. We did not have family financial help for him, and loans were not much of an option in those years. I was able to go to school for two years thanks to my parents and I got a two-year degree in Preschool Education. My ex got into Medical School, and I went to work as a secretary. His school was only a two-year school, so when our son was three years old, we put him in the back seat of our car and drove to the mid-west for the last two years of medical school. We had a few boxes shipped to us, bought garage sale furniture, and lived in government housing. I was unhappy in the marriage but also had hope in the future that things would improve. We lived in government housing with one car. My ex continued to throw fits of rage and to be verbally explosive. I thought that this was just a phase that we were in and that my ex would calm down eventually when he didn't have so much stress at school. Plus, I was used to it.

I babysat for the next two years and our second child, a girl, was born when my ex was in his third year of medical school. After I had this beautiful child, the hospital provided a candlelight dinner for me and my ex. I was so excited as this was so special. Except that he didn't show up for the dinner. I was devastated and embarrassed. He showed up the next day and told me he had been having margueritas at another medical student's house to celebrate! The tone was set that he was not going to be available anymore. His focus was on his career and his patients, not on me or the children.

I set up a home day care with preschool activities in the apartment so I could be home with my children. I became pregnant with our third child at the end of medical school. Depression visited me again, as I was in a second story apartment, babysitting, with no car in a terrible cold, dark winter. I left the apartment twice a week to go to the grocery store and to church. We had no extra money and went out once a year to a movie. Poverty is not fun. I had thoughts of jumping out the second story window. But I was pregnant, had two other kids, and knew that God was there for me.

We moved to another state for his internship. He decided to specialize in orthopedic surgery. I begged him not to choose that specialty, as I knew it was hard on a family and marriage. He ignored me.

I don't know if he cheated on me or not, but I had suspicions. A few memories stand out. When I was nine months pregnant with our third child, he started his internship. He was invited to a get together for the Interns and Residents. I didn't know it was a party with nurses also. This is way before cell phones. He didn't come home until 3:00 a.m. I sat by the window waiting for him and crying. He was stinking drunk. He called in sick the next day as he had a terrible hang over. I don't know what happened at the party.

I had our second daughter, third child, at the beginning of that hard year. She was such a gorgeous baby. During my labor, my ex spent the whole time visiting other patients and my attending doctor sat in the room with me. This was to be the story of the rest of my marriage.

The internship was demanding as my ex was at the hospital for thirty- six hours and home for twelve hours to sleep then back at the hospital for another shift. My kids were six years old, eighteen months and newborn. I remember wishing that I had three dollars extra each week, so that I could take the children to a church sponsored babysitting event once a week for one hour. I had no breaks.

A very difficult thing for me to share is that the ex used pornography. It upset me when he had porno magazines in the house, and I would ask him to throw them away. We were barely making it financially. We would eat at the hospital on Sundays as they had free dinner for the interns' and residents' families. I saved fifteen dollars that year from my babysitting to buy a cheap bathing suit and material to sew two T-shirts for myself. I then found porn magazines that he had bought hidden away that cost twenty-two dollars. I was heartbroken that he had spent money on porn. The porn then became more hidden, but I would find magazines stowed away occasionally.

After his one-year internship, we then moved for his three-year residency in orthopedic surgery. His anger and rages increased. He had problems with other doctors in the program. He almost got kicked out of the Residency. My ex was a very believable liar and belittled what I was going through. He would tell me what I was feeling, or thinking wasn't important. (Although his was.) He denied that I felt what I felt, that I knew what I knew, that I heard what I heard, or saw what I saw. This was a continuation of how my mother and father treated me when I was growing up. Perhaps this is why it was so difficult to accept the reality and make good decisions that would have been healthy for me and my children. I remained in a state of confusion and indecision. And I was very trapped financially.

During the residency I worked as a medical secretary for a year and then was able to go to college for a short time. There were some highlights as we bought our first condo, sold it after a year and bought our first house. I loved the house was furnished with dark brown carpet and gold furniture, the décor of the day. It was 1977 after all! My son's room was decorated with a car bedspread and the girls had pink bedspreads. I had friends in the neighborhood and friends that were other resident's wives. I loved taking my girls to preschool at the university and attending classes. I wanted to go to law school, so I took Poly Sci classes. That dream never came to be. I loved my little boy, and he went to school across the road next to an almond grove. We had a cat that was part of the family.

We went to church occasionally but never really became part of a church family. I remember going to a church service where the pastor was teaching about dying to self. (Luke 9:23 ESV) "If anyone would come after me, let him deny himself and take up his cross daily and follow me." I sobbed through the whole church service. People around me were concerned for me. I couldn't even talk. I felt dead inside and felt like the "me" was dead. I felt like I had lost myself. The verse was not about my internal state at all but that is how I interpreted it. I was depressed. I then went to see a doctor that I had never seen before. His solution for me was that we needed to take a vacation. We had no extra money to take a vacation and my ex had no time off. I needed counseling but it wasn't anything available to me. So, I carried on as best I could.

When I was twenty-six, during the first year of my ex's residency, my mother was diagnosed with breast cancer. She had a mastectomy, but it had spread to her lymph nodes. A year later, the tumor reappeared on the incision of her mastectomy of her left breast. My mother and I had become close as adults. She had asked Christ into her life as her Savior. She treated me with respect and as an equal. Our relationship was healthy. She had quit drinking. When her cancer spread, I was so upset I didn't have a period for five months. I had to decide if I really believed in the story that Jesus was the son of God, that He died and was resurrected and that He ascended into Heaven. Was heaven where my mother was going? I decided I did believe that Jesus was who He said he was. I had always believed and prayed to Him, but this was different. It was a heart change. I knew she was going to die. But I knew that Jesus was real.

In 1979, after residency, we moved to the southwest, as my ex owed the Air Force two years payback for two years of medical school tuition. I was twenty-seven years old. My mother was dying. My children were nine, five and almost four. We were invited to a couple's Bible study by a neighbor. I also joined a women's Bible study. I asked Jesus into my life as an adult at the women's Bible study. I wanted to be with Him and to serve Him and know Him. I had done this before at age eight, and I was recommitting myself to Him. My ex accepted Him also, I think, at the couple's Bible study. My mom was dying from cancer, and the Lord gave me strong Christian support from my Christian friends, and also from some wonderful neighbors. Our kids played together as we lived in the same neighborhood. We were in a gourmet group and belonged to a country club with a pool. We had a nice house, and my kids were happy in their school and home. I didn't work for those two years, the only time I had off from working until I was 65 years old.

I never shared my marriage issues with anyone. My ex-husband continued with his raging and fit throwing at home and his constant complaining about his colleagues. By then I wanted out of the marriage, but there was no money. I felt I had no way to support the kids on my own. I wanted to keep my kids safe, and I didn't want to go on welfare. They were my focus.

My ex's pornography use was hidden, but I will share something that I think was related to his pornography use. He wanted to have anal sex with me. The magazines that I had found earlier during the internship had portrayed that act. I told him no and to go find a gay person to do that with. He quit trying to get me to engage in that. However, several times he wouldn't take no as an answer from me when he wanted to be sexual (normal intercourse) and persisted in groping me even though I was saying no and pushing him away. I felt pressured to have intercourse against my will and gave in as he wouldn't take no for an answer.

My ex was an orthopedic surgeon in the Air Force, and he refused to follow an order from the head of his department. He was nearly court martialed. I was a wreck. My Mom was dying, and my ex was in trouble because of his attitude and actions. He was ordered by the Air Force to see a psychiatrist for a year. I didn't see any changes, and I think he convinced the psychiatrist he was working on his issues. Looking back, the only thing that kept saving him from total disaster over the years was that he was an outstanding doctor. He was very intelligent and provided his patients with excellent care. His personality problems prevented him from reaching his full potential.

A very dangerous pattern of thinking was happening with me, as I would repeatedly tell myself, "It will get better when…" I thought things would get better when he got out of medical school, then when he got out of internship, then when he was done with residency. Then things would get better when he was out of the military. He always had a good excuse or explanation as to why he had conflicts with others. I then thought private practice would solve the ongoing problems. Little did I know that the environment or situation would not change the life I was living. My belief that he would change never materialized. I was not being honest with myself about what the reality was. I wanted to be a doctor's wife, and I sacrificed for it! And I never wanted to live at poverty level again. The carrot at the end of the stick was what I was focusing on – not the reality of the stick that was making me tired and anxious. I weighed 98 pounds. I wasn't anorexic. It wasn't a body image issue. I was just very stressed and really couldn't eat much.

My mother died in March of 1981. I was twenty-nine. My ex got out of the Air Force in September, six months after my mom died, and we moved to the western United States, where my family lived. When we moved, my ex managed to insult the other doctors in the new town, so he was not invited into a call group where they shared coverage and had time off. He had no call coverage, and thus had to be available all the time for on call emergencies. He had so many issues with the other doctors that the next six years were full of strife. He had no time off and we rarely went out of town. We had to take separate cars wherever we went. I managed his medical practice and filled in as needed for work as a receptionist, nurse, biller, etc.

The money situation improved after a few years, but I found I was pregnant with our fourth child. She has been a total blessing. The other kids were fourteen, nine and eight years old when she was born. I wanted to go back to college, and I wanted to leave the marriage. My ex had gotten more emotionally abusive, and his rages were increasing. He was drinking more and more. I cried a lot but got up each morning to take care of the kids, the practice, the house, the dog, and the car. No one took care of me. He was unavailable. But I still believed his claims that he was the best orthopedic surgeon in town, and that the doctors were jealous of him. I wanted to believe it, as I felt trapped with the responsibility of four children.

We had our first vacation when I was thirty-one and had been married for fourteen years. I was about five months pregnant with our fourth child. Somehow, he convinced another doctor to cover for him so we could leave town. We went to the Cayman Islands. It was wonderful being at the ocean in the tropics. I snorkeled and swam and enjoyed the beautiful landscapes. The day before we were to return home, I had a breakdown and started crying. I did not want to go back to the stresses. We were going back to where I was on my own most of the time. Since he was at odds with the doctors in town, I was being ostracized also. I was running his office and had the stress of that. Plus, I was having a difficult pregnancy and had trouble with a varicose vein that was causing lots of pain. As I was crying, he decided he wanted to have sex. I was so upset. He didn't care that I was crying. Instead, he laid on the bed next to me and started to masturbate while I was laying there sobbing. I ran to the bathroom and closed the door while he finished masturbating. He hadn't cared that I was upset. He only wanted to have sex. It was all about him.

I was so humiliated. He didn't care about me. But I was pregnant and felt stuck. I continued enduring him and his behaviors. I concentrated on the children. I was pretending as I was starting to die inside.

Shortly after that and before the baby was born, my ex got a vasectomy. Six hours after he got home, he started drinking. He was also on pain medication. It was snowing outside. After dinner, I realized he was gone, my son was missing, and the car was missing. I had no idea where they were. This is before cell phones. They showed up an hour later. My son had driven (fourteen years old) since my ex was too drunk to drive and had plowed the car into a curb in the deep snow. My ex was wearing his bathrobe. They made it home, but both tires on the left side of the car were destroyed. They had gone to buy ice cream.

My new baby was delivered. It was an easy delivery, and she was a beautiful baby. When she was a few months old, I invited my ex to come home on his lunch hour. His office was five minutes away. I prepared a nice lunch. He never showed up and he never called! He said a patient had come in late, so he had stayed to see her. She had big boobs that he admired. He always criticized my small breasts. Soon after, I found a T shirt in his office from her that said, "A Hard Man is Good to Find". He denied that anything had gone on. His wanting to have anal sex, wanting me to get bigger boobs, and insisting on having sex when I was an emotional wreck, were all signs that something was very wrong. I will never know what he was up to, and I guess it is best if I never find out!

One evening later that year (1984) when I had gone out somewhere, he beat our third child so hard that her entire bottom was black. He did this because she couldn't swallow a pill whole! I should have left him. My ex was the big important Christian Doctor. I was very alone. I couldn't tell anyone about the beating or other experiences. Now I know I should have reported him to CPS and filed for divorce.

As I write this, I wonder why I didn't escape the ongoing unstable behavior that was resulting in anxiety and confusion in me. He blamed me for our issues and blamed the doctors in town for his conflicts with them. I believed him. I lost sight of what is "normal" and what peace, love, and kindness looks like in a marriage. Why didn't I leave? I feel stupid now. But I had endured fifteen years of psychological and verbal abuse and threats, so at this point I was extremely psychologically battered. This is hard to explain but it is a state where my self-esteem was destroyed. I was told that I wasn't important, what I said or felt wasn't important and I was traumatized by his loud anger, scary body language, and emotional and verbal abuse.

I was also very fearful. I was stuck in the pattern of pretending that all was well, as I desperately went through daily life. It took years and an anti-depressant for me to pull out of the chronic depression and anxiety I was experiencing, which had developed into PTSD. Emotional and psychological abuse is almost worse than physical abuse, as they mess with the mind and soul. My body was telling me that I was in an unsafe relationship. I was being incongruent, which means that my outward appearance did not match my inward appearance. It is difficult to leave when you are battered psychologically. It is like asking a cripple to run a 100-yard dash. It is impossible. Later, when I became a therapist, my specialty was trauma and abuse. I understood it and knew it took time and healing to move out of it.

I was ignoring the signs. Please – if you are reading this and you are experiencing verbal, psychological, physical abuse or if your children are being abused, don't ignore these very critical signs. Go get help to get out of the situation and into a safe place. Bring these things into the light of Christ. Don't hide them. Tell someone the truth of what is happening. Go to counseling. Get help. You will probably need help getting out of the situation. Ephesians 5:11 &13 (ESV). "Take no part in the unfruitful works of darkness, but instead expose them… But when anything is exposed by the light, it becomes visible…."

I became involved with Christian Women's Club. I had many Christian friends with this group of Christians, and it was a safe place (even though I told no one what was going on). I eventually became a speaker and traveled giving my testimony of accepting Jesus as my savior to clubs in the area and out of state. God had

His hand on me. However – I will say I wasn't being honest about my marriage and my situation. I pretended all was good. I suppressed my hurt, pain, and confusion. The problem was that I wasn't being honest about how my marriage really was. I had it hidden. I spent a lot of energy being a Christian to others and to trying to keep my children shielded from my ex's raging attacks.

This is called whitewashing in the Bible. Mathew 23:27 (ESV). "…For you are like 'Whitewashed tombs, which outwardly appear beautiful, but within are full of dead people's bones…" The outside looks fine, new, and pretty but the inside is a mess. That is what I was. Whitewashed on the outside to look good to others, while inside I was dying and rotting away. It is also being dishonest. I was telling myself that I was OK and that my ex was OK. I suppose it was a way for me to get through my days. I would desperately pray to God and read the Bible looking for answers. Somehow it was all my fault, and I was the one with the problems. I wasn't being honest with myself, but I knew deep down that something was very wrong.

I started thinking about divorce again when my fourth child was about four months old. I had been a practicing/seeking Christian for five years and struggled with "was divorce a sin and would God forgive me?" I was worn out. We had been at poverty level for many years and there was finally a good income from his practice. I could start thinking about getting out. But my plans went sideways when my sister invited us to attend a Christian marriage seminar. It was a weekend of Christian ministry for marriage. (Later I realized that Kirk was at the same marriage seminar and was a speaker!) I heard the message that you stay married for your lifetime. I learned lots of skills to stay in the marriage from the seminar. My ex learned a few and used them to appear to be more considerate of me for a short while. I was a casualty of some fundamental Christian teaching that you can only get a divorce in cases of adultery. (I now know pornography use is adultery.) So, to follow the Christian teaching and honor God, I stayed in the marriage. I regret this so much now as I look back. I realize now that I also was very worried about my kids and what a divorce would do to them. I would search the Bible for answers. I always got the verses "God hates divorce." Malachi 2:16 (ESV).

I walked with God, attended church weekly, and was involved in Bible studies and church ministries. The pastor of the church I was attending stated often that "You must stay married no matter what." I was very sad inside and suffering in an unhealthy way. I thought I was protecting my children, but they were being affected also. God kept His hand on them and me and brought us through it somehow!

Over the next eighteen years I struggled with staying married or getting a divorce. The issues I contemplated were huge in my mind. Born again Christians are faced with many challenges concerning divorce. The teachings of the Bible are that God hates divorce. Jesus said divorce is only ok if there is infidelity. Mathew 5:31-32, (ESV). He said that if a man divorces his wife and if she remarries, she is committing adultery. A believing Christian who wants to please God and follow His edicts is put into a very precarious position, if he or she is in a marriage marred by abuse (physical, mental, psychological, and or sexual), addictions, or even adultery. It is hard to be honest about what is really happening.

Ephesians 5:22-32 describes a marriage in which the wife submits to the husband and the husband is submitting to Christ and the husband is treating his wife as Christ cherishes the church. The marriage vows between a couple, creating a covenant before and with the Lord, promise to love, cherish, and honor each other. All of these elements: Christ's teachings, God's stance,

Ephesian's definitions of marriage and the marriage vows all need to be carefully considered in the issue of divorce. And lastly – is the marriage of the heart or on a piece of paper or both? Does it make you a prisoner of the law with no love or respect, or is it a union of love in the heart?

God looks at our hearts. He saw that the love I had for my ex in my heart was pretty much gone. Marriage is of the Heart – two people who are connected in their hearts and souls with God involved. 1Samuel 16:7 "…For the Lord sees not as man sees: man looks on the outward appearance, but the Lord looks on the heart." (ESV) I was not being truthful, as I ignored my true feelings. God saw where I was, and He saw me coping with this difficult marriage and the wish to be out of it. But the belief that I had to stay in it no matter what kept me in the marriage and in misery.

Jesus said that divorce is only allowed in cases of infidelity. What is the definition of infidelity? Is it cheating sexually while married? Is it having an emotional affair? Is it using pornography to reach climax without your spouse? Can infidelity be defined as being in a relationship with someone or something other than your spouse? How about putting your spouse aside to spend hours shopping the internet, being on social networking, or being married to your work? Infidelity breaks the soul and spirit connection of the spouses. Israel's adultery was of the heart to other gods. It wasn't physical adultery, but spiritual adultery, when their love for God was gone, and they turned away from Him. And then, God divorced them. Jeremiah 3:8-10.

Another issue I struggled with is, what other actions break the marriage covenant. Do abuse or addictions break the marriage covenant? Abuse takes many forms. It can be emotional abuse, physical, sexual, or psychological abuse. Does abuse break the marriage covenant? Abusive behavior is not cherishing, loving, or honoring the other person. It is not respecting the other person. In fact, it is harming the other person. I now believe it breaks the heart bond between the two spouses. It kills the trust.

Addictions also contribute to breaking the marriage vows. When a person is addicted to alcohol, substances, pornography or gambling, that person is in relationship with their substance or behavior. The marriage of the addicted person is to the addiction. Time, energy, money, and thoughts go to the addiction, not to the spouse or marriage. Is this a form of adultery? I believe so.

And lastly, children need to always be considered in a divorce. Will the divorce harm or help the children? My experience as a counselor showed me the following: Children also suffer when parents are experiencing severe marital problems. They suffer even though the parents might think they are protecting them by staying married in spite of the marital problems. Divorce can negatively affect children if the outcome of divorce is poverty, loss of relationship with one of the parents or the parent's family (grandparents, etc.), or instability of one or both parents. New partners of either parent can affect the children negatively if they are abusive or neglectful. Divorce can be positive if both parents can effectively co-parent and remain stable and constant in the child's life. Divorce can be positive if the conflict between the parents resolves through the divorce, and the parents move on to a healthy lifestyle.

And so, my processing staying in the marriage versus divorce continued. I wish I had some of the wisdom that I just shared with you earlier in my life! I was stuck in "God hates divorce." Now – on to my story of staying in a difficult marriage after the marriage seminar in 1985.

My ex finally antagonized the whole medical community in our community by telling a patient to sue one of the local doctors in front of staff and other doctors. This broke the doctors' code of "don't report each other". I went to a Christmas tea for the Medical Wives Club shortly after that, and not one person would talk to me. I was humiliated and embarrassed. No one would sit with us at medical dinners. We were being shunned.

We moved to a larger neighboring city in 1987. My ex could not continue to practice in the small town due to the conflicts he had with the other doctors. I was thirty-six years old. He got in a Call group in town and had a solo practice. My self-esteem was practically zero by then. His demeaning treatment of me and the stress of his inability to get along with people had taken its toll. I was literally crawling through life with no energy. My joy was in my children. He continued to be irresponsible and would not shoulder the weight of the family or the running of his practice. He never took responsibility for his behavior and justified it in his mind. He was not able to process the negative feedback he received from colleagues and coworkers. But he did well with his patients, and they loved him. I really wanted Jesus to come back and relieve me from my exhausting life.

I continued managing his practice. I had two teenagers at home and a four-year-old. My son stayed with friends in our former town for his last year of high school and then went away to college. We didn't want to move him for his last year of high school. I desperately sought God and His wisdom. I did everything I could to stay in the marriage. I accepted blame for things that were not of my doing from my ex. I guess I wanted to believe him when he made excuses for his behavior. I would say this – when a pattern of behavior continues despite consequences – there is a problem. I was torn between what I needed and wanted to do (leave) and what I thought I had to do (stay married no matter what.)

I was a five-star codependent. There are many definitions of codependency The one that applied to me the best was putting other people's needs and wants ahead of your own to your detriment. It is actually a form of addiction, as it numbs a person to their own hurts and pain. Instead of dealing with my distress, I concentrated on other people's issues and became a super helper and nurturer. The problem with codependency is that people will kick a codependent in the teeth, as over time they resent the excessive helpfulness. There is a lack of respect for the codependent that develops. Plus, the codependent is not addressing his/her own very deep seated, painful issues. It worked to keep me stalled and unable to move forward. Robert Hemfelt, Frank Minirth, and Paul Meier, *Love is a Choice*, (Thomas Nelson, 2003).

I thought I was protecting my children, but I now see that I damaged them by staying. I wasn't able to protect them from their father's erratic behavior. The children were so precious to me. I would insert myself in between him and them so that his attacks were directed to me. By then, my ex had developed a drinking problem. He would come home and drink four or five beers right away. I also found out he would also put wine in an emptied beer can, so I had no idea how much he was really drinking. He later quit drinking for a few years when I threatened to go to Al Anon. He didn't want his addictions to be public. My nightmare was hidden from sight, and we looked like a perfect Christian couple.

I went to a Christian counselor when I was thirty-eight years old, after twenty-one years of marriage. I went mainly because my brother, Bob was spreading terrible rumors about me, my ex and my son. I had various people tell me what he was saying. Unfortunately, what he was saying wasn't true. He was right, in that there were problems, but what he was saying was made up. Remember, this is the brother who specialized in spreading falsehoods when he was a child. He never tried to help me or support me. He fed into the problems my ex had with the local doctors and went into the attack mode since he was very social in the community and was embarrassed by being related to my ex and me, I think. If he had talked to me, maybe I could have been honest about what was really happening. His friends called me "the evil sister" because of what he told them. There were other things he probably said about me - like being stupid (which I was!!!). Unfortunately, this derailed me for years, as I focused on him and the attacks instead of being honest and focusing on my marriage. I felt assaulted from all sides.

When I was seeing a therapist for help, the counselor was not able to get me to fully open up about my marriage. My ex was a prominent physician and a Christian doctor. We went to the same church as the therapist. I was not able to talk about the verbal and psychological abuse that was still ongoing. I was not able to talk about the addictions that my ex engaged in. I was caught in the Christian myth that we are to be perfect (what an awful place to be stuck!), and marriage is something you must stay in. My childhood had taught me to "just deal with it", don't complain and that my own thoughts, hurts and needs were not important. But the counseling helped me start to climb out of a deep depression, and I started to get back to who I was. I actually had to stop and ask myself what I was feeling when I was upset, to name the feeling, and to feel it for ten seconds. I had suppressed my feelings so much that I wasn't feeling them anymore. I cried often, and the only emotion I experienced was being very sad. I didn't even feel angry. I was confused also, as my ex would tell part of the story and then would twist it to suit him. I didn't know what to believe.

At age thirty-nine in 1990, I went back to college (my youngest was seven) and got a degree in English Literature. I had waited until she was in first grade, as someone had to be there to raise the kids! The dream to go to law school died as there was no local law school. I wanted to teach High School English, so I started on a teaching track. One of the courses was Introduction to Counseling. It changed my course of study. I applied and was accepted into the master's program for counselling. I think I was drawn to the counseling program as I unconsciously was trying to figure out what was wrong with me and my life!!!

I wanted a divorce and had wanted one for many years. But I was still going to the church where the pastor preached, "You have to stay married, no matter what." I would search the Bible for answers and always found that God hates divorce. I believe that God hates divorce because it can cause many problems for people and that it is a decision that should not be taken lightly. At that time, I didn't realize that pornography use was a form of adultery. I read books on the subject of Christian divorce and the effects of divorce on children and thus stayed in the marriage even though I felt that I was fighting to stay healthy. I knew I was miserable, but I told myself that I should be grateful, as I had so much materially, and other people weren't so fortunate. And I had children that I didn't want to expose to a divorce.

One incident in my first marriage illustrates the ongoing instability of my ex's behavior. We were on vacation with the youngest child at a fast-food restaurant. She was nine. We were in a long line and had picked out our orders. When we got near the front, my daughter changed her mind. My ex threw a fit – he yelled loudly, stomped about and left in a rage. He drove off in the rental car and left us there! This is before cell phones, so we were stuck. We had to sit there in embarrassment for about an hour until he came back. These repeated episodes put me in a constant state of hypervigilance. In so many instances I could not fight back or take flight, I could only freeze. Freezing is what I had learned to do when he threw fits at home or in public. He was very loud with aggressive body language. My reaction of course, had started in childhood when my mother would rage, and I would freeze.

"Freezing is fight-or-flight on hold, where you further prepare to protect yourself. It's also called reactive immobility or attentive immobility. ..., you stay completely still and get ready for the next move." "Fight, Flight, Freeze", Healthline, accessed on November 7, 2021. https://www.healthline.com/health/mental-health/fight-flight-freeze Maybe that is part of the reason I did not leave the marriage.

Another memory I have of this time period is when my ex got arrested in Disney World. Yes, he was arrested in Disney World! We were on a family vacation in Florida. He got angry because a woman had cut in line in front of him, and he started yelling and poking her in her chest with his finger. He was arrested and held in Disney World security for three hours. I am not making these things up! Who gets arrested in Disney World?

His constant anger continued. He always blamed others for his ongoing issues and never looked at himself. It was always someone else's fault. And remember, he was mandated to counseling for a year when he was in the Air Force. Later, in 1992 and 1995, he was ordered to a year of counseling by his call group. I think they recognized that he was a talented physician, but had personality issues, so they tried to get him help. He did not use the therapy sessions to work on his issues. He knew how to behave to keep his colleagues from totally kicking him out of the call group, although he was a constant source of irritation. He even would weekly go through the call schedule and complain about it.

I finally learned to distance myself emotionally. I would watch him throwing a fit with a loud angry yelling and aggressive body language. Instead of soothing him like I had been doing all those years, I would think, "He is acting like a two-year-old." I was gradually being released from the bondage of his behavior and my fears. But my heart would sink, and my stomach would tighten when I heard the garage door open as he came home. I never knew if he would come in and throw a fit or not, so I would prepare myself to not react. I was still trapped from what my church taught; you must stay married no matter what. I guess even if it kills you.

Now you know why I stayed. My childhood had conditioned me to accept verbal and psychological attacks. I would freeze or try to calm my mother down. This behavior transferred into my marriage, and I eventually developed depression and anxiety and PTSD. This interfered in my ability to make decisions. How did I stay? By focusing on the kids, my school, and God. Thankfully my ex worked a lot and was gone a lot of the time. Putting on a front that everything was normal also helped. I eventually started setting strong boundaries with my ex. In fact, setting boundaries kept him from being so aggressive towards me.

At age forty-four, I graduated with my master's and started a private practice specializing in Christian counseling. I was pretty good at it, since I had lots of skills. Because I was able to stay in my own dysfunctional marriage, I felt I could help others do the same! I actually thought I was doing the right thing and worked to keep couples together. My beliefs and my adhering to the church's mandate were very strong. Although I did not encourage people to stay in physically abusive situations. I wish I had listened to myself!!

As I pulled out of the depression and trauma, I started to get stronger. I began taking some anti-depressants which broke the chronic depression and anxiety so that I could begin healing. I did all I could do to stay married. I prayed, read books, and stuffed my pain. I entered personal counseling again and did some EMDR for trauma. EMDR is a therapy that moves the traumatic memories from the emotional (limbic) part of the brain to the cognitive (prefrontal cortex) part of the brain so that a person isn't trapped in the trauma any longer. The EMDR helped me to not be so reactive to his abuse. I had a session of EMDR where my body shook for an hour, and this released the anxiety and trauma that was stored in my muscles. I then became trained in EMDR and trauma work. EMDR and trauma counseling became my second specialty. Francine Shapiro, *Eye Movement Desensitization and Reprocessing*, (Guilford Press, 2018).

Now I was waiting until the last child left for college to finally get out of the marriage. I still believed that I needed to stay married for her sake and stability until she was in college. And perhaps this was true, as she is a very stable adult.

An example of how I was finally coming out of the depression and PTSD was how I handled my ex as he was having a rage attack and threatening to leave. Before, I had always backed down so he wouldn't leave, and he would calm down. (This is from years of me being manipulated by this threat and also from my mother threatening to send me away when I was growing up.) I didn't back down. Instead, I got a suitcase and told him to pack and get out. He didn't leave and never threatened again. (I had endured twenty- six years of the threats to leave – if only I had known.) What a shame he didn't leave.

I didn't love him and did not want to be married to him. The spiritual and emotional bond to him was gone. I was married on paper and was walking through the motions of being married. If I tried to talk about my feelings or concerns, he would tell me it wasn't important and he would brush me off, or he would get angry. He hid his behaviors behind being a "Christian doctor" and also by being married to me, the Christian wife and counselor. And he refused to go to marriage counseling!

In 1998, when the three oldest kids were out of the house, he confessed that he had been going to the adult bookstore downtown to go in the booths and watch porno films. I was mortified. His pornography addiction was out of control for a respected doctor to engage in that behavior. He claimed he had now stopped going to the adult bookstore. How horrible that this had been going on.

In 2002, my ex was mandated by the three hospitals he was affiliated with, to go for a psychiatric evaluation, and he was in jeopardy of losing his license to practice medicine. Nurses at all three hospitals had complained about his rude, degrading behavior. He originally told me he was going for two weeks to a clinic for physicians to work on his anger problems on his own, as he knew he needed to get help. But then it came out that he was ordered to go. I had lost all respect for him, and I couldn't stand him at all. I was finally living with my eyes wide open. SEE IT FOR WHAT IT IS – NOT WHAT YOU HOPE IT TO BE! You can have lots of excuses – just don't use them! Be honest.

My youngest daughter was graduating from high school and would be going out of state for college. It was time for me to move on. Kirk's divorce would happen many years after mine.

Chapter Nine

Surfer Dude

KIRK'S DECISION FOR DIVORCE

About three years before my divorce, I began to accept what God wanted me to see. My relationship with Him began to get better. And then, after He brought Deborah into my life, my relationship with Him became more real than ever before in my forty-eight years as a Christian. Vibrant! I have been set free in Christ in my heart from so many years in prison mentally and emotionally. And He has spoken to us so many times. His Spirit has been so present in our daily lives it is amazing. I often tell Deborah, "I now know what God intended marriage to be!" "If I were to die tomorrow, I am grateful that I have experienced this wonderful union, a man and a woman in love as God intended." It is fulfilling, enriching and comforting beyond words.

I had decided I was really going to get a divorce. It took a couple of years to get to this place, but I was finally ready, and the marriage was over. We were married on paper only, not in our hearts or in our relationship. It had been over in our hearts for many years, we had just not acknowledged it. God was giving me freedom in my heart.

Over the years, for about twelve actually, my path would briefly cross Deborah's. We knew of each other, and thought highly of each other, but did not really know one another very much at all. We actually came pretty close one summer when I was sixteen. I had just gotten my driver's license, and a friend of mine and I drove to the lake to visit my aunt and uncle who had a cabin there. I had been there before, years earlier, and my uncle had taken us out on his Chris Craft classic boat. I had jumped into the lake from the boat and still remember how cold the water was! On the trip we camped out a few miles from my aunt's cabin for a couple of weeks. We cooked on a camp stove, mostly canned stuff, and smoked Tarrington cigarettes. We were all grown up, you know, and that is what grown men did, smoke cigarettes. I think the reason my folks let me do this at age sixteen was that my dad's sister's cabin was there, and we agreed to check in with her. Which we did and we received a nice meal for stopping by. Deborah was fifteen at that time and spending her summer at the lake on the other side of the lake. If we had only known! I would have driven over to see her, and she would have taken her dad's boat over to see me. Who knew we were so close and that both of us loved the lake!

On that road trip I got my first traffic ticket…. for going too slow! That was embarrassing. Teenage boys are not supposed to get tickets for going too slow! Driving through the mountains, I noticed a cop a few cars behind me in my rear-view mirror. Being a new driver, I slowed down and purposely stayed under the speed limit. He pulled me over and said I needed to pull off when too many cars got behind me, something I did not realize. I guess the line was quite long. But no one was honking, so how was I to know?

Deborah had been my wife's therapist and had also walked with us through my son's divorce, which was very difficult.

Deborah had been a great support for my ex-wife. It had been a number of years since Deborah had spoken with my ex-wife, but I knew she knew her pretty well. So, on a couple of occasions I had asked Deborah if she could help my ex, or how I could help her. I respected Deborah greatly, and had no conscious feelings toward her at all, but I did think she was cute. A few years before my divorce I had shared with Deborah concerns over my wife once again and also shared with her the progress I was making with family relationships, and friends which had been lost over the years because of my difficult marriage. For some reason, my ex would always find a reason to terminate relationships with our couple friends. One person would say or do something that was normally extremely minor, and that was the end of it. As time passed, I would periodically think of Deborah fondly and counted her a dear friend. Again, fully conscious feelings were not in play, yet. I must confess that my comment of "I count you as a dear friend," was a feeble attempt at flirting. So feeble that she never even recognized it!

Then, by what we have come to know as God's planning for us, things began to change. I had been in a dry and unhappy marriage for many years. Intimacy had nearly completely ceased many years earlier, without my consent. My marriage relationship was damaging my life and I was not being refined by the normal challenges of a marriage. I decided I could not live that way any longer and was going to seek a divorce. I began telling my ex-wife that we would both be better off divorced. This started several years prior to the divorce. And we were even looking for houses to live in separately. This was a difficult decision for me. An earth shaking one really. I had the religious belief that one should never get divorced. I must stay where I was until death, no exceptions except adultery. We had attended marriage seminars on several occasions that taught this concept.

The teachings on how a marriage should be resonated with me deeply. But in reality, it takes two people to make a marriage work. And when one person is not willing, or able, or is not capable of working on a marriage, it simply cannot work. Some people have emotional or mental handicaps which simply prevent them from participating in marriage as God intended. It can get very complicated, but the final verdict is that it takes both husband and wife committed to each other to make a marriage work. I don't think my ex and I ever had a real marriage in the sense that it started with emotional trauma and my taking the role of co-dependent. It continued in this fashion through kids and grandkids with drama, emotional turmoil, dysfunction and challenges. Looking back, it wasn't a marriage, but a misguided relationship which was so out of balance from day one that it would never work, without killing me! As I look back, there were elements of a normal marriage, but the out of order portions far outweighed those, at least to me.

Most churches and marriage seminars teach that you should stay married no matter what, with very few exceptions. This is terribly burdensome for that one who knows they are in a broken relationship and need relief. It is like telling someone suffering from constant physical beating to simply stand there and bear it, instead of escaping. This can lead to hopelessness and despair. However, God has a broader view of things that we do. He helped me to see that in the realm of the body, soul and spirit, there are many different forms of adultery and unfaithfulness. There are many types of abuse, not only physical. If one is being damaged, rather than refined by circumstances, then one should seek to get out of the damaging relationship. When a person is suffering from physical ailments from the stress of a relationship with emotional and mental trauma, or PSTD symptoms, staying is foolish and damaging. When the heart of a spouse is divorced from the other for reasons of addiction to drugs, alcohol or other addictions like gambling, pornography, hoarding/shopping, or there is emotional or physical separation, it is time to seriously think of leaving and facing the reality of the situation.

For most of my Christian life, forty-five years, my thinking was rigid concerning divorce. I couldn't even pray about it, because I thought God would be angry with me for bringing this subject before Him in prayer. I thought about discussing it with him often, but simply thought I couldn't. He would be angry with me. (As if He didn't know what I was feeling and thinking! Pretty stupid of me for sure.) But, when I finally did, He met me with a loving and understanding heart. This may sound controversial to some who read this story, and how He worked with us may not be how He wants to work with you. But our story is what happened to us. If you hold the belief that one must stay married regardless of the situation, then perhaps God will help you soften your position after reading our story. If your spouse is addicted to porn, then perhaps you should consider that such activity is adultery. If both spouses are being refined and not damaged, then perhaps you need to hang in there and make it work. However, when a relationship is harming a person or damaging the person through abuse verbally, emotionally or physically, I believe God cares more about the person being harmed than the institution of marriage. Think about that for a moment. If divorce is the ceasing of abuse, isn't it good? If it is the ending of unwarranted emotional pain and suffering, isn't it good? If it is the beginning of happiness, and hope for the future, isn't it good? When the pain and anguish reach a point of damaging us, we should allow ourselves to tell God, "Lord, I can't take this any longer. Help me find a better path. Help me accept the fact that this marriage is broken and damaging."

We cannot flourish if we are in a toxic or non-healthy

relationship environment. Think of yourself as a flowering plant or fruit tree. If a plant is located in a place where it cannot flourish because of too much or too little sun, or because of soil conditions not conducive to growth, or where there is not enough water, then it cannot do well. It will not fruit nor bear beautiful flowers and will never grow into its intended potential. So too, if we are in an unhealthy relationship, we will never come to the full stature of being what God intended us to be. We will not have the fruit in our lives that can bless others, and we can fall short in our conduct and behavior, which will then produce negativity instead of blessing. Be honest with yourself about where you are planted.

The understanding which helped set me free from the prison of religious thinking was a scriptural overview summary of marriage, not a specific passage of scripture. In the Old Testament, it started with Adam and Eve as man and wife. Then later, men had many wives. David, a man after God's own heart, had many wives. And it was God who told David after he had Bathsheba's husband killed, that He would have given David more wives. It is the same God who loved David and Solomon, who both had many wives, who loves us today. He has not changed. He was not against multiple wives. Shocking? Perhaps to our modern-day religious thinking, but not scripturally shocking. Today, it is customary to have one wife. In eternity we are told there is neither male nor female, and there is no giving in marriage. There will be no man and wife relationships in heaven. The Church is to be the bride of Christ, of which we are part. So, the end result of all we experience here on earth is to prepare us for our eternal state of existence, as individual members of the bride of Christ. Marriage is not the end all institution for men and women. God will end all such marriages as we know them when we are in heaven. Call it the Great Divorce ceremony if you will, but all individual marriages will end, and we will all be wed to Christ as His bride.

Scripture says that there will be no giving of man and woman in marriage in heaven, and that there will be no male nor female, but we shall be as the angels. (Luke 20:34-36; Gal. 3:28; Matt. 22:30) So spiritual maturity and eternal health are God's goals to perfect His bride and transform us into His image. If what we endure here is harmful to that end goal, and is damaging to our eternal health and maturity, it can and should be changed. I am not speaking of the challenges of being refined and made perfect, but rather getting out of enduring things which are damaging or stunting to one's growth in the Lord. There is a great difference between enduring the refining of God through other people, including our spouse, and being damaged or mistreated.

In Jeremiah 3:8 and Isaiah 50:1, scripture states that God gave Israel a certificate of divorce and put her away. **God had a divorce!** It was because Israel's heart had turned away from Him. They did not have intimacy of the flesh with another God (husband), but their hearts had turned away from Him to worship other Gods and to rebel against His laws. In this case, the "adultery" was that of the heart, not the body. If God had a divorce because the heart intimacy was not there and was polluted, must we stay married in similar situations where the relationship is dead, the heart of the spouse is elsewhere, and the marriage in the heart is over?

I reached a place of deep peace about the divorce and moved forward in that direction. Then, Deborah came into my life a little bit at a time, but not until I had decided I was getting a divorce. I had to make that decision first, for then God was free to show me what was next. Deborah was not the reason for my divorce, but slowly came into focus after my decision. Once I made the decision to leave, God started moving, and His presence in my life came alive! In Ezekiel chapter 37, there is the vision of an entire army of dead dry bones coming to life. Well, that is what it was like when I finally decided to leave, everything in my life came alive! It was just as dramatic as the army Ezekiel saw coming to life. Out of the death of my imprisoned marriage God brought new life! Deborah's separation and divorce took place thirteen years before mine.

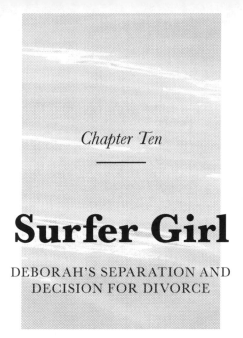

Chapter Ten

Surfer Girl

DEBORAH'S SEPARATION AND DECISION FOR DIVORCE

I finally separated in 2003 when my youngest daughter left for college. I had become mean toward my ex after his revelation in 1998 that he had been going to adult bookstores. I felt disgusted. I was done with him and his behaviors. I am ashamed to admit that I was impatient, angry, and demeaning towards him. When anger and demeaning behavior is poured into another person's heart – that person can become bitter and angry and start to sin also. And I was sinning. I then started to think about suicide. I thought about stockpiling pills. Being a counselor, I knew this is a warning sign. I decided it was time to divorce rather than kill myself. Suicidal thoughts are often escape thoughts and they have to be taken seriously. My situation was dire and beyond anything I could tolerate.

I was finally free from him when I separated. I skipped in joy. But I was separated for two years as I carefully prepared for divorce. I was afraid of my ex and his anger and did not want a messy divorce. I knew it could have been a huge court battle, and it would have been ugly.

The church I had gone to for twenty years was not there for me after I separated. The head pastor acted like he had never seen me before in his life. The college pastor, who I had served under, called me on the phone three times to beat me over the head with the Bible. I did not share with either of them about the details of my marriage, and how I was dying in the marriage. They didn't ask why I was leaving either. The final time the college pastor called me he told me how divorce hurts everyone – the kids, the grandkids, the grandparents, aunts, uncles, friends, and the church family. I finally said "But what about me? Don't I matter?" He never called me again. Only one woman reached out to me from all my friends and church family of over two thousand people. Only one!!!

The Christian church I was attending fundamentally taught that people should stay married no matter what. This can be common in other churches also. If a person decides to get a divorce because the situation is so miserable, the church many times will judge that person to be out of God's will. How terrible. How cruel. Many times, the person is criticized, ostracized and is deemed unwelcome in the church. This happens so often. And sometimes one partner will say grievous things about the other to entice the church leadership and members in taking sides. Rarely do the leadership and leaders come alongside the divorcing partners to help and pray. This is amazing, considering that Christians have a divorce rate of over 50% in first marriages. How many Christians are out there having lost fellowship with their church families and are being judged cruelly by those who have no idea of what the divorcing person has endured?

This is a travesty. God loving Christians will fight for their marriages and will stay in them until they are at the point they will be destroyed if they stay in the marriages. Often the partner who is no longer caring for the other gets a free pass. The abuser, cheater, addict will use their partner and will seem to be innocent when the spouse leaves the marriage. This person can even be an elder, a professional well thought of in the church, a stay-at-home Mom, a Christian doctor or a very good liar.

I came to a new conclusion about divorce. The marriage covenant can be broken by abuse, infidelity, neglect, or addictions. It can be broken by the true state of the heart. If a person isn't married to their spouse in the heart, then the reality is, there is no marriage. God divorced Israel. Why does God hate divorce? Because it is not His heart's desire, He knows it comes from pain, sin, evil and darkness, abuse and unfaithfulness. But He divorced Israel because it was the just consequence of their actions. Sometimes divorce is necessary! (Isaiah 50:1 and Jeremiah 3:8)

About this time God said to me, "I have seen everything - I have seen it all. Everything will be fine." God does see everything. Nothing is hidden. He was telling me that He saw my pain. I had been praying for the gift of speaking and praying in tongues for several years. I felt that my communication with God was blocked, and I wanted to be in closer contact with Him. I had also experienced spiritual warfare and oppression during some counseling sessions with clients and felt I needed more protection. One of my clients prayed with me and I was flooded with the Holy Spirit and received the gift of tongues. I have heard God so much more clearly since I was given that gift. It is a wonderful help in prayer.

During the separation, my ex ended up in a lawsuit with another doctor in town. The jury ruled that my ex was liable for damages and asked for a list of all of our assets to award to the other doctor. I made the list and then went into my closet and got on my knees. I gave the list to God and told Him tearfully that if

He was going to take everything away from us (me) that I would accept His decision. I had prayed many times in the past on my knees for God to deal with my ex. The next day as I went to court to present the list, the judge reversed the ruling. We could have lost everything, but God protected me! I filed for divorce shortly after that and was free, for the first time since I was seventeen years old, from the oppressive anger, rages and irrational behavior. It was 2005 and I was fifty-four young years old. I had finally been truthful with myself about the fact that I was not married to my ex in my heart. It was only a paper marriage. The connection had been gone for years. Sadly, because of my inability to be honest about myself and the marriage, we had both experienced some miserable years. Our children had also been damaged. God knew exactly my heart condition as He looked at my heart.

After my divorce I was very unsettled. I was happy to be free from my ex, but my family was gone after all those years. My foundation was gone. My kids were all mad at me – even though they had seen me enduring the attacks, the mistreatment and dishonesty. I had moved to the lake and was isolated without family. My friends had deserted me (a single woman is a threat to a married woman I guess). I didn't share my story, as I had seen people in my church take sides in divorces, and I had seen some of my clients torn apart by the church. I was disillusioned with the church and the teachings of the church.

One of the sad results of a divorce is that children can become estranged. Sometimes it is the ex who turns the kids against the other parent. This is called parental alienation. My ex traumatized the children when they were growing up. One of them is still traumatized. She has anxiety related to his outbursts. They were angry about the divorce, as my ex had blamed me for everything and told this to the kids. My daughters and I are reconciled now. My son has never forgiven me and hasn't spoken to me since the divorce. I take responsibility for being angry at my ex the last few years we were together, and I know this affected my son, as he was living with us at the time. No matter how many times I have apologized, my son will not forgive me. He sees me as evil and being unfair to his dad. My ex has continued to blame me for all of his problems and unwise decisions since the divorce fifteen years ago.

My son also suffered growing up by my codependency and overparenting. I tried to help him too much, especially as a young teenage and college age boy. I haven't shared with him or my daughters much of what I am sharing in this story.

A wise person told me that in my marriage, I was like the little Dutch boy who was holding his finger in the dyke to prevent it breaking and flooding. That is what I was doing. After I removed myself from the marriage, the dyke broke and my ex started down a path of self-destruction, unstopped. Eccl 10:8,9 "He who digs a pit will fall into it and a serpent will bite him who breaks through a wall. He who quarries stones is hurt by them, and he who splits logs is endangered by them." (ESV)

After the divorce, my ex, at age sixty, ran off with a twenty-one-year-old who worked in his office. He sold his million dollar plus practice for $30,000 (including the furniture and equipment valued at $90,000). He moved out of state and eventually lost an office building he got in the divorce. He bought his girlfriend a boob job, a Jaguar, and put her through nursing school. He paid all her bills. He had several jobs, not having success in staying put very long, and then got a job in a different state. (His girlfriend had dumped him by then.) He was then fired from his last job and lost hospital privileges. A repeat of years earlier, as he was just not able to address his own issues. His angry, disrespectful behavior finally caught up with him at age seventy. He blames me to this day for his consequences, although I had nothing to do with any of them. He will not take responsibility for his actions. I now know that God wanted me to be out of the marriage, as my ex was not walking with Him. My ex looked very Christian to the public but his heart was not godly. He did not grow in humility, charity, grace, kindness. He was proud, angry, spiteful, jealous, and cruel. Bad fruits are listed in Prov 6:17-19 as "…haughty eyes, a lying tongue…a heart that devises evil plans…" (ESV)

AFTER THE DIVORCE A CONFUSING NEW LIFE

After my divorce, I started dating a bit and found that it was a scary dating world. I didn't know the dating rules of 2005 and I had been married since I was 17 years old. I felt I didn't need a Christian man, as my ex claimed to be a Christian, but his actions did not reflect it. I was disillusioned with God and the church. I felt that following the church rules hadn't brought about the life I had prayed for – one of a happy marriage and peace. I made a choice to go into the secular world even though I still believed that Jesus was my Savior and I prayed constantly.

I experienced something I call the Divorce Crazies. This is when a person gets a divorce and does things they wouldn't normally do. I did things I am ashamed of now. It was like I was living my young adulthood that I had missed in my now fifties. I even got a boob job since I was insecure about my small breasts!

My best advice to a newly divorced person is wait on the Lord. I charged full steam ahead and went into a long dry period. I met someone, became engaged and was in a relationship for eight years. I lived with the person, and it was so out of God's will. I was in rebellion. I was in a place where I was discouraged and disappointed in God and the Church. He did not bless that new relationship. The fiancé was not a Christian and I was in the desert spiritually. Hebrews 3:12-13. (ESV) "Take care, brothers, lest there be in any of you an evil heart, leading you to fall away from the living God. But exhort one another every day, as long as it is called "today", that none of you be hardened through the deceitfulness of sin." I tell people now not to ever live with someone. The commitment is weak, and it is difficult to disengage from the relationship. It is out of God's will. He tells us not to do sinful things because He loves us and doesn't want to see us hurt. I hurt myself and others around me by being in that relationship. I was very unhappy. The ex-fiancé never bonded with my kids or grandkids and that ended up being a blessing, as they didn't miss him at all when it was over.

I had repeated my pattern of being trapped – this time I was trapped in sin by being in the live-in situation. I also was repeating my pattern of thinking things would get better. My body was telling me differently. While in this relationship I had high blood pressure for which I had to go on medication. I developed GURD (indigestion issues), a mold reaction, and a severe eye infection. I was trapped in the snare of the devil due to not listening to God. But God did help me recover myself from the snare of the devil as He says, "God may perhaps grant them repentance leading to a knowledge of the truth and they may come to their senses and escape from the snare of the devil, after being captured by him to do his will." 2 Timothy 2:26 (ESV).

There was no excuse for my behavior. I knew it was wrong to live with someone. I knew it was against God's principals. Romans 1:20 "...So they are without excuse. For although they knew God, they did not honor him as God or give thanks to him, but they became futile in their thinking, and their foolish hearts were darkened." (ESV).

So of course, the "living in sin" relationship I was in died. We had nothing in common, and I spent time alone on the weekends at the lake or with my kids. I began to spiritually look to God again and prayed for Him to get me out of the relationship and that I wanted to be with a man of God. A true man of God, not a pretend one like my ex. There are consequences to sin. Don't think there aren't! I lost eight years of my life. They were ill spent years, and they were spent in the desert. Psalm 68:12" God settles the solitary in a home; he leads out the prisoners to prosperity, but the rebellious dwell in a parched land. "(ESV)

I finally broke off the relationship and bought a house sight unseen near my daughters. I was done and decided I didn't want to have another relationship and just wanted to live in my little house, alone. I should have made this decision eight years earlier. I thought about moving out of state, but decided to stay where I was for two more years and bought the office building my office was in. At one point after I left the relationship, I was asking God why I had gotten into the relationship in the first place. He told me I had disobeyed him. Simple answer, but it shed light on what I had done.

I finally was at the end of my rebellion and wanted to be right with God. The lesson is to put God first and wait on Him. He knows what is best for us. Jesus died and rose again so we could have abundant joy in life. It is amazing what God does when we finally give up our desires and wants and let Him take over. He blessed me beyond anything I could have imagined. He brought Kirk into my life. I repented and He received me back with open arms and blessed me beyond my wildest dreams. 1John 1:9 "If we confess our sins, he is faithful and just and will forgive us our sins and purify us from all unrighteousness." (ESV)

I will tell anyone not to ever live with someone without being married. It is a sad path to be on and it is difficult to get off the path. If the relationship isn't healthy and happy enough to solidify with a marriage contract, then it isn't the correct relationship.

Chapter Eleven

Surfer Dude & Surfer Girl

KIRK – FOCUSING ON DEBORAH

Deborah and I began to communicate about family, our personal interests, and had several months of periodic light and friendly talks and texts. As we did, I came to realize in my heart, "Hey, I could really have a great relationship with a woman like Deborah." I loved the way she thought. I fell in love with her mind first before anything else. After the divorce terms had been agreed upon and signed, I decided to pursue a relationship with Deborah. I was falling in love with her mind, her thinking and talking, and wanted to pursue more of a relationship with her for sure. I remember having not one doubt about our future relationship. I had determined to pursue her, and never doubted. Normally, in a new relationship there is hope and some doubt or concern that things may not work out. I never had that with Deborah. I was going to seek her, and inwardly there was no fear of failure. None!

I had reconnected with an old High School friend and was leaving for a ten-day surfing trip to Hawaii. My second of the winter. On my first trip, I had decided to seek a divorce, but no one knew except me. It was on that trip that I began texting some with Deborah. We had some wonderful sharing on a very platonic level, but sweet and heartwarming. She was beginning to come into focus! During the time between surf trips, Deborah and I had many times of sharing and talking. We were surely warming up in our relationship. It was wonderful!

We met over coffee several times, and our discussions deepened. We were not dating, but we were talking with each other. We were getting to know each other better. I would come to our meetings prepared with a short list of questions or topics to discuss or disclose. Being sixty-five years old, I did not hesitate to ask questions important to a marriage. And I wanted to disclose to Deborah all of my shortcomings, at least all the ones I knew about. I told her of my hairy chest and back, and actually showed them to her. She gently reached out and touched my back. I remember how special that felt. I still do, to this day. I asked her to smell my breath, yes, to smell my breath because I wanted her to know about me, and my ex had complained about it, probably another excuse to not have intimacy. She said it smelled fine, like coffee. That was a relief. I told her I had dry hands; a bit rough. She felt them and said they were nice. Another thing my ex had used as an excuse for no intimacy. Deborah said that when she touched my hand, she felt electricity! Wow! That was a confirmation of the chemistry we had together.

On our first get together, I had brought her a latte from Starbucks. As I waited for her in the front area of her office, I set the latte and my coffee on the counter. When she opened the door, I spilled the coffee all over her office wall. She had just purchased the building two days earlier. She happily replied, as she laughed, "You baptized my office." She was not upset at all. And afterward said that it actually made her feel at ease, because she was nervous about meeting me to talk. However, this is not the end of the "baptism by coffee" event. As we both kneeled down to clean up the mess, her shirt came up a little above her pants. And the top of her bottom was showing. It was so cute and attractive I had to look. Then I told myself, "You shouldn't be looking" and I would look away. Then I would look again, and again tell myself the same admonishment, "You shouldn't be looking." This repeated itself at least three times. I was very impressed with how cute she was, and how in shape she was. God was giving me just a little preview of her physical beauty. I knew she was beautiful of heart and mind, and now I knew she was physically too. Wow! That little portion of her behind is now affectionately known as "the coffee spot."

We continued our discussions and covered everything we could think of that was important to us and a relationship. "How do you feel about certain types of sex in marriage? Is oral sex okay with you? What is your opinion on anal sex, which was a definite no for both of us!" "What do you like and dislike about intimacy?" Yes, we got right down to the details of intimacy. Deborah asked if I did porn. I said I had seen it but did not do porn. That was important to her, rightly so. Her first marriage had been negatively affected by her ex's porn addiction. We both believe it is a clear form of adultery. We discussed finances, family priorities, faith in God, and our basic beliefs. We covered in a matter of weeks what many couples take years to discuss and address. We had both been married, and knew what we wanted, and what to ask each other. We discussed religion and politics, and found we were likeminded in both of these areas. Another wonderful fit.

I had learned a song to sing for Deborah. Izzy's "Somewhere over the Rainbow." She was my motivation for learning the song, which had sat on my piano for a few years to be learned. I felt

Deborah was my "dream come true" and for her, I wanted to learn it and sing it to her. She cried as I sang it to her …. "Dreams really do come true." We were seeing it clearer now. We knew God was weaving us together. It was amazing how well we bonded and felt so comfortable with each other. It was as though we had known each other our entire lives. I shared another Christian worship song, in Hawaiian and English. Deborah paused and asked me if I minded if she sang in the spirit (in tongues) while I sang, as she didn't know the Hawaiian words. I stopped cold and froze, looking at her in amazement. I had wondered if she was spirit filled and was taken back in shock and delight at her question. I said, "You pray in the spirit!" Oh, how wonderful, I had no idea you were a spirit filled believer," as was I. Yet another piece of our union we shared together.

DEBORAH– KIRK COMING INTO MY LIFE

Kirk appeared out of the mist on his Surfboard!!!! I didn't expect that God would bring me such a man of God who I can worship Him with. God redeemed me through His Grace. Only God could have arranged my relationship with Kirk.

I had been Kirk's ex-wife's counselor years before. She did phone sessions with me mainly about issues with her daughter. I met Kirk at the son's divorce hearing when I went at his ex's request in 2005, when I was newly divorced. I thought he was very handsome and nice. They seemed to have a strong marriage. I had several counseling sessions on the phone over the next year or two with his ex and sometimes Kirk was on the phone also. Then six years passed. Kirk called and asked for an appointment to get help for his then wife. He described behavior that was abnormal. I did what I could to get her to see her doctor and to see if she wanted to start counseling again, but she said no. I was disappointed that I hadn't been able to help her, and that I hadn't been able to help Kirk.

Kirk came in for advice about a year or so later, because he felt I knew enough about his wife to offer some guidance. His then wife had cut off his daughter, son, and the grandkids. He wanted some guidance as to make sure his granddaughter could go to a private high school and also wanted to reconnect with his family. He shared with me that his marriage was difficult and that it had always been difficult. He was married for life and couldn't leave because of his relationship with God. He also talked about how he was a surfer and had some trips planned, but that his wife would punish him when he went on the trips. I felt desperation for him to be able to live, as he was being suffocated. I related. As we talked, I felt a huge PING! It was like a current of energy that surged through my whole body. Something connected for me and I was extremely attracted to Kirk. I couldn't show it. I kept my poker face as my body went wild. He left and I was flabbergasted. In over twenty-one years of counseling, I had never been attracted to a client. I was so careful to stay professional. I prayed to God asking what to do and He told me to "do the right thing." So, I did nothing. Kirk was married and had told me he had to stay married. And anyway, I couldn't date a client until two years after the counseling ended as per my ethics and licensing.

I thought about Kirk often after that. I had a crush on him. He had a place at the lake in the next bay from where my house was. I would stand-up paddle board in that bay often and looked for Kirk hoping to see him out on the lake. I never ran into him. He sent me some texts of him playing in the lake with his grandchildren as he had reconnected with his family. I was happy for him. He later sent me some pictures of his grandkids cooking with a chef. Again, I was happy for him and responded appropriately. He sent me a few more pictures and said he counted me as a dear friend. Since he was off limits, I didn't think much of it. He later told me he was flirting with me as his divorce was happening, but I thought he was just being nice! At this point I did not know he was getting a divorce.

In January 2016, I was in the process of buying my house and office. I had ended the other relationship and I was in Hawaii on one island and Kirk was surfing on Kauai. Kirk started texting me about Hawaii. I texted him back and asked if his ex was coming to Hawaii. He let me know they were done. He then sent me a picture of him on the beach with his surfboard and board shorts. That was it for me! It was game on. I had feelings for him that I had stuffed. I sent him a picture of me on my Stand-up Paddle Board. We had fun texting. In February, Kirk asked if we could have coffee when we were both back home. He was in the final stages of his divorce. I, of course, said yes. I felt confident about meeting with him. And over two years had passed since I had seen him as a client.

I had closed escrow on my office two days before Kirk was scheduled to bring coffee to my office. I was nervous and at peace at the same time. I saw a white Expedition backing into a parking space and somehow, I knew it was Kirk, even though I had never seen his car. He came into the office carrying two large cups of coffee. As I greeted him, he went to put the cups down on the check in counter and the largest spilled all over the counter, the wall and the floor! It broke the ice and I told him he had baptized my office. We laughed as we cleaned up the mess. Our first coffee time ended up being us sharing our views on God, being Christians, and talking about our families. He gave me a book that he had written. I felt so comfortable and happy. We connected spiritually.

Kirk would come every week to my office for two hours of coffee and conversation. He brought notes with questions listed to ask me. I had questions for him also. We discussed our past experiences, our challenges, and our future dreams. One day Kirk came in bringing a guitar. I wondered what he was going to do. I didn't know that he played the guitar and had a beautiful voice. He sang to me "Over the Rainbow" by Izzy, and told me he had learned it just for me! I loved it and was so touched. He also sang worship songs, most of which I didn't know. I asked if he minded if I sang in tongues so then I could sing with him. He was shocked and pleased that I was Spirit filled like he was. We shared so many details with each other and we had agreement on our values and beliefs. He did decide to share some details with me about himself physically. He had two fingers severed in different accidents and they had been repaired but were a little shorter. I touched one finger and felt an electricity. He also showed me his hairy back. I touched him on his lower back and told him it was indeed a hairy back! He also told me he had hearing aids. He was so handsome I didn't care at all. I told him I previously had breast implants and had them removed. So much for baring it all! After we were married, Kirk often tells me how much he loves my breasts, just as they are. He thinks they are beautiful!

After a month or so, I knew I was in love with Kirk. As I drove into the office on a day when we were going to meet, I decided I needed to tell him we could not have physical contact until his divorce was final. When he came into the office, the first thing he said was that we could not have any physical contact until his divorce was final!! We were on the same page, and we still are!!!

We continued to interview each other, and Kirk had many lists of questions. I wish we still had those lists. As time went on, he asked me personal questions. Did I like oral sex? What about French kissing? I told him what my sexual boundaries were. I asked him the big question in my mind – do you use pornography? No, absolutely not, he said. That would have been a deal breaker for me. Our sexual boundaries were similar. We were both in our sixties, so we cut quickly to what we wanted to know about each other. I didn't see any red flags. (I still don't see any five years later!)

We discovered something else we had in common. In 1984, when my fourth child was a few months old I wanted to get a divorce. But I attended a marriage seminar where Kirk, my future husband, was a speaker with his wife. I stayed married for the next 18 years, because at that seminar I was taught Christians cannot get a divorce. Kirk bought into the same message and had stayed in his marriage 43 years, even though it was a miserable one also. Too bad we weren't able to be honest about our marriages and our hearts all those years ago. Maybe God would have connected us sooner. Sometimes we think we are in God's will even when we are living sad, difficult lives.

Kirk's divorce was on track about the same time I finally got to move into my new house. He called me and said that his soon to be ex had suffered a minor stroke and was in the hospital. The divorce might not happen right away until she was OK. I told him I would wait for him if it took six months or a year. He called me a few days later and told me how his ex had demanded he get her out of the hospital. She said, "Get me out of here now!" The discharge process was taking so long that Kirk and his son had wheeled her out in a chair, were stopped by security, and then she was discharged by the doctor a few minutes later. His ex wanted to sign the papers for the divorce and her new house that day. The attorneys came to the house, made sure she was coherent and of sound mind, and the divorce papers were signed.

Kirk was free, as was I. Finally, after years of bondage and heartache we were both free.

Chapter Twelve

Surfer Dude

KIRK, BACK TO HIS DIVORCE STORY

Well, back to my pre-divorce story. As I came close to the divorce being final, I was still being haunted by what I now see as my "prison of religious thinking". I became concerned about the wonderful love and feelings I was having toward Deborah. Was it okay to have these feelings prior to the divorce being recorded? The terms of the divorce had all been agreed to in writing and were final, but the divorce had not yet been finalized. I was troubled. Deeply so. I took this to the Lord in prayer one night. My cries for Him to help me were from the very core of my being. In great turmoil and tears I cried out to Him, "Lord, I have these feelings for Deborah, and I am not yet officially divorced. (Although I had lived many years as a single man in a dead marriage, which was a form of divorce for sure) I do not want to do anything that would offend You or cause You to remove your favor from my life, or bring shame to Your name." I poured all of this out to Him and placed my love for Deborah on the altar. He could tell me whatever He wanted to as I lifted it all up to Him. Then, as though I were watching a big screen TV, He said to me several things. He said, "I brought her early." I melted in tears, overwhelmed with His words. He had brought her into my life prior to the divorce finalization. He had done that! Looking back, I think He brought Deborah early because I was so done with the marriage, and yet trapped in it by my thinking, that I had seriously thought of having an affair. I needed a relationship with someone desperately. I thought about having an affair often, but never did it. I think God knew that bringing Deborah early stopped me from thinking about having an affair. Then He said, "Because you have been faithful and endured." He had seen my years of pain in my marriage, and He understood. He told me Deborah would be a comfort for me. His kindness flooded over me, and I was lost in tearful gratefulness. He knew He was bringing us together and where we were going. With God and in the spirit, there is no time, so He allowed this to comfort me. His kindness was overwhelming.

He went on to say, "She will be a healing blessing to your family." As I write this now, she has truly been a healing blessing to many in my family. God knew! In my forty-four years of seeking His face as a believer, I had never had a time with God like this. I did not deserve His kind thoughts toward me.

God went on to say that because I had stood for my family, attempting to normalize relationships, He would stand for me. He had seen my efforts. The fact that He was aware of everything I had done, and aware of my prayers and concerns, made me realize His great love for me. It was a love I did not deserve but was so very grateful to have. I was also concerned about my business and the impact the divorce might have on it. He said he would take care of that and that He would preserve and bless my business. I expressed concern about finalizing the divorce and He said, "I will take care of it." This time with God went for three hours, as I was comforted by Him, and expressed my gratefulness to Him.

My relationship with Deborah was from Him, and I knew it with every atom of my being.

As the time grew close for the divorce to be finalized, my ex-wife and I were a bit stressed, and things were a bit rough between us. Divorce is a difficult thing, even when two people are working together to make it happen. My ex-wife and I had wanted a non-contested divorce, which we had. But even then, it was very rough. We each needed our own attorney and with attorneys, things can get difficult to say the least. They seemed to try and undo agreements we already had in place, had agreed to and reduced to writing. I had decided to give my ex the maximum she could have received had we fought in court. I was advised I could probably do better and give her less, but I felt it was worth not going to court in a battle. In the end it worked out fine, but there were difficult and stressful moments. This can happen even with a non-contested divorce.

When I boarded the plane that year for my second surf trip to Hawaii, I felt like the divorce settlement with my soon to be ex-wife was on shaky ground. I was very worried and burdened. Things were not good. Everything had been agreed to for quite a while, but as the date of final signing came closer tensions rose. On the plane, I had the chance to read a book about Deborah's father and his life story. I couldn't put it down. It made me want to live along side of him during the experiences he recounted as a rancher and sheep herder. It was a comfort to me in a wonderful way. And it gave me great insight into Deborah's family. Something I greatly appreciated and respected. Reading his book on the plane helped me step away mentally from the divorce and was a welcomed diversion.

Anyway, I was still worried deeply as we landed in Hawaii. Five hours of cell phone silence. What was the status of things with the divorce, I wondered? Little did I know how much

God had been doing in those five hours! He was very busy. As I switched my cell phone off of airplane mode a host of text messages flooded my phone. My ex-wife had found a house she loved. She and my daughter had looked at it together. She wanted to put an offer in on it as part of the divorce settlement. As we were not yet divorced, she needed my consent to do this. I texted back, "Yes! If you want it, go ahead and put in an offer." She had transitioned into the future planning of her life without me and was totally excited about the house. The five hours of silence were all it took for God to move things forward. Everything was on track. The offer was subsequently accepted, and the house was going to be hers. And it was. A huge burden was lifted off of me at that moment, before I even got off the plane.

My old friend met me at the baggage claim. As we waited for my surfboards and bags, we began to talk. I shared with him the divorce status. I shared how all of the terms of the divorce had been signed and agreed to and how God had done a major thing while I was on the plane. When I boarded my ex was in a mess emotionally and was talking of derailing the divorce. But during the flight she had found a home that had propelled her forward into now really wanting to finalize the divorce. I also realized how I had never been that important to her. It was only my provision, and my constantly fixing her emotional flare-ups and enablement of her lifestyle that she really wanted. I was just the vehicle for her to have that. I was her "binky". For her to get this amazing home was all she needed now to move forward, and I had nothing to do with it. God had done all of this while I was flying for five hours in a no communication zone!

I shared with my friend how Deborah had come into focus in my life and the details of our forming relationship. We both cried as we felt the presence of God in our sharing together. His reply to me was, "You're walking in a miracle." He shared how he and his wife had known and seen the challenges in my marriage better than I did. He was greatly supportive, and a comfort to me. For one hour we sat on the ledge in front of the airport, basking in His love and the wonderful things He was doing. It was sweet!

This was not the first airport encounter he and I shared. As I previously shared, much earlier in our lives, when I was twenty years old, I gave my life to Jesus over the Christmas holiday. I began to send my friends Gospel tracks and share with them in letters about Jesus and salvation. Months later, after being saved and before I flew back to Hawaii, at one of the prayer meetings I had gone forward to stand in prayer for my friends in Hawaii. I asked God to save them. Then, a few weeks later I flew back to Hawaii. My old friend and several other friends met me at the airport. They were all grinning in a very abnormal way. What was going on, I wondered. It turned out that the very night I had stood in prayer for them, my best friend had been saved. A friend had come over to where he and I lived and had shared Jesus with him. He recounted how at the time he was drunk and had also smoked a great deal of marijuana and smoked some hash. He was out of it! When this friend told him of Jesus, the Lord touched him, and he was instantly sober and of clear mind! That was the hand and love of God! Then, my other friends were saved also, accepting Jesus as their Savior. When they told me this, you can imagine the wonderful presence of God surrounding us as we rejoiced in what He had done. Amazing! I think God loves airports!

So, here I was, again in an airport in Hawaii, having an experience with this dear friend and God. My trip was blessed, and my texting with Deborah continued, as we were falling deeply in love. The more we shared, the more I knew she was sent by God to me. This dear friend became a casualty of my divorce in the long run. A story I will tell later.

Last Minute Roadblock

The attorneys had drafted all of the previously agreed upon terms into the final documents. Signing was scheduled. Everything was ready. Then, two days prior to the signing, my ex-wife had a minor stroke. This was her second over the past ten years. So, into the emergency room we went. She was kept in intensive care for the night and was to be dismissed the next day to general care, as she was recovering well. Both her first and second strokes had been very minor in nature with no long-term damage, fortunately for her. The move to a general care room was delayed because of a lack of beds and so one more night in intensive care was planned. This was to be followed by one night in general care, then home. Because of this I thought the official signing of the divorce documents was probably not going to happen. In fact, Deborah and I had talked after my ex was admitted to the hospital, and she said, "If it takes six months or a year, I will wait for you." I had gone home that night thinking, "This divorce will not happen for many months." I was reluctantly resolved to that fact, although saddened by the thought of having to wait, as Deborah and I were already emotionally bonded. There was nothing I could do. It was totally out of my hands.

My ex wanted to sign, and she really wanted the escrow on her new home to close as well, which was part of the final documents to be signed. She did not want her stay in the hospital to delay anything. So, I said, I will have the attorneys bring the papers to the hospital if you want, to which she responded, "Yes!" But I was not sure the papers would really get signed, given the situation.

The night before the scheduled signing, my ex was moved out of intensive care and down into a general care room. They finally had an open bed. At 5:00 a.m. that next morning, my ex called me and said, with clarity of mind and rock-solid determination, "You come get me out of here right now!! I won't stay here one more minute. I want to go home!" She was not saying this because of the documents to be signed, but because she hated being in the hospital. She had a very bad night of sleep with the groans and noises of other folks and staff, and simply insisted that she wanted to go home - NOW! So, I called my son, asked him if he could meet me at the hospital, and away I went.

When I arrived, my ex had packed up all of her belongings, was sitting on the chair next to her bed, and was ready to leave. I asked for the nurse, and she came in shortly thereafter. During the brief wait, my ex was insistent on "get me out of here." "I want to go home." When she saw me there to take her home, she had started to grab her packed belongings and was determined to leave immediately. The nurse came in and said it would be best if my ex stayed another night. I asked her if she would do that, suggested to her that it would be best, but she refused and said, "No, I want to go home." Come what may and no matter what was in her way, she was leaving that hospital, and soon.

After an hour or so of waiting for discharge papers, and being given the run around, I said to the nurse, "Please bring her a wheelchair and I will take her home." She said sure, but no chair ever came. They were waiting for the doctor to give her one final exam before departure. At this point, my ex was adamant, and wanted to go. She would wait no longer. I took an office chair with wheels, placed her in it, and my son and I proceeded to roll her down the hall. She had a weakened left leg, which she thought was from the previous stroke. But the doctor said that was not the case, as that was not the area of the brain mildly affected. Anyway, a wheelchair would have been helpful in getting her to the car, but a chair with wheels would suffice.

Well, this didn't set well with the staff, and security showed up around halfway down the hall. Then, all of a sudden, the doctor, who was "too busy to come because he was making his rounds" showed up. My son proceeded to tell everyone that his mother could go home if she wanted, and that they have no legal power to prevent her from leaving. They concurred. The doctor repeatedly said, "Just go back to your room and I will help you once I am done with my rounds." My son again said, "My mom wants to go home, and you can't stop her." There was a lot of tension in the air. You could feel it and cut it with a knife. I think my son was madder than I was at how we were all being treated. I had already explained to the staff that I had arranged twenty- four/seven in home care through a licensed agency to assist as needed, and repeated that again, giving them the name and contact at the agency. This helped some. Then, as though God had tapped the doctor on the shoulder, the tension in the air ceased and he said, "Oh, okay, I guess I can ask you the exit questions right now." He sat at the computer, which happened to be right where we were standing, and proceeded with the discharge procedure. Ten minutes later we were on our way home. And, the attorneys were on their way there too, as my ex had requested and was relieved to know. She wanted that house! The signing was going to happen! And not only did a wheelchair arrive, but a person also came with it to push it while I got the car. Much better than an office chair with wheels!

When the attorneys arrived, the one thing my ex wanted clarified was, "I am going to get the house today, right?" She wasn't upset about me leaving, but she sure wanted that house. It didn't have bad breath or rough hands, I guess. And I was exiting a dead marriage too! All in one day.

It was God who had moved my ex to call and ask to come home! He has ways of working things out that we could never imagine. From a reluctant acceptance of the fact that the divorce would likely be delayed for some time to a final signing was a major turnaround in one day. It was as though the moment I let it all go and said, "it's out of my hands," He made it all happen.

My Dream Girl

As I mentioned in the beginning of my story, since I was sixteen years old, I have had a deep yearning for a special girl to share my life. In my longings she would ride with me in my Volkswagen van on surf trips, travel with me to Hawaii, and together we would share life. This longing was very deep, strong and lasting for my entire life, but the fulfillment of this longing was elusive and never came about, until Deborah! Deborah was that girl! As our discussions grew, and as we shared our hearts, I saw in her so many wonderful things. She was smart! She was very caring. She was a woman of great stature in her heart and mind. She was like-minded with me in so many ways it was amazing. And she was the most beautiful woman in the world! I did not have a list of things I was looking for in that special girl to share my life, but when I saw them in Deborah, I then knew what they were. She was more than I could have dreamed for. More than I could have imagined to ask for. She was the girl that should have been in my VW van with me. I tell her often, as we enjoy various events in life together, "You're my VW van dream girl." We have wooden surfboard shaped wall hangings that say "Surfer Dude" and "Surfer Girl".

Chapter Thirteen

Surfer Dude

KIRK – OUR FIRST DATE

We did not have our first date until after my divorce was final. It was at an Easter Sunday brunch after we had gone to church. We went to brunch at the lake at a very nice lake front restaurant.

It was our first date, the first time I had held her hand, and our first kiss. I had sent a gift box to the restaurant for the hostess to place on our table just before we were seated. This took a bit of coordinating. And since the gift was jewelry, I had sent an empty wrapped gift box for the table. As we were seated, Deborah was delighted by the gift box. When she opened it, there was a note saying, "Ask Kirk what was supposed to be in the box." She did, and I then took the real gift box out of my coat.

She was overjoyed with the thoughtfulness, and I was thrilled by her happiness. It was a charm necklace with charms representing individual things we had learned we loved, that represented what we had talked about, or what she meant to me. It was all amazing. After brunch, we walked outside. We were at the lake, on a beautiful windy day, the lake was dark blue, as were her eyes. We held hands and kissed for the first time under the towering pines on the beach. A really wonderful kiss! We both loved the lake, and the moment was magical. We were on our way toward marriage, and I think we both knew it.

Deborah shared with me something that had happened to her a few years earlier, when I had spoken to her about her thoughts for helping my then wife. Deborah told me that she had a very strong "ping", as she puts it, experiencing a very strong attraction and feelings towards me. So much so that she had to ask God what it was about and what she should do. He said to her, "Do the right thing." Which she did - which was ... nothing. She waited and wondered.

DEBORAH OUR FIRST DATE

Our first date was a week after his divorce was final on Easter Sunday. I wondered how it would go and if we would like kissing each other. I was in love with him but didn't know about the physical part. He took me up to a very nice restaurant on the lake for brunch. It was a windy, cloudy day. We sat in a beautiful spot overlooking the lake. I saw a little box sitting in the middle of the table and he told me it was for me. I was expecting some chocolates. I opened it and there was a card that said to look in Kirk's pocket for the real gift. I did and was so amazed to find a Pandora necklace and bracelet. He had charms on the necklace that symbolized us – a palm tree, blue for The lake, a dolphin, a guitar and music notes, a bird, a D, and a K, a heart with a key to his heart, and a rooster! He was a romantic! What an amazing man. He was a devoted Christian, was kind, smart, and handsome, could sing, play the guitar, write songs, was an author, and a successful businessman. He was a true Renaissance man. He paid attention to what I loved, and he listened to me! And we connected. The kiss came later on the beach, and it was beautiful. He also was a good kisser!!!! And he smelled delicious – our pheromones matched.

But we had a rocky week the next week. My ex-fiancé caused some uproar with me and Kirk's ex was moving out of his house and into her new one. We had a misunderstanding and Kirk showed up at my door with a bouquet of flowers and wanted to talk through it! I had never had anyone do that for me before. I had always been left with hurt and had to deal with it myself. We talked through it, and I knew Kirk was a very kind, caring, healthy man. A breath of fresh air!

Chapter Fourteen

Surfer Dude

KIRK AND AN OLD TESTAMENT WEDDING

The very first wedding recorded in Scripture was this: "And the rib that the Lord God had taken from the man he made into a woman and brought her unto the man." Genesis 2:22. (ESV). God simply brought Eve to Adam. Years later in Biblical history we read about Isaac and Rebecca's wedding: "And Rebecca lifted up her eyes, and when she saw Isaac, she lighted off the camel.......... And Isaac brought her into his mother Sarah's tent, and took Rebekah, and she became his wife; and he loved her: and Isaac was comforted after his mother's death." Genesis 24: 64-6. (KJV). There was no preacher and no paperwork - simply God, the man, and the woman.

In times of old, it was very common for older men to marry younger women. As is done sometimes in our society today. I have fun sharing the story of how Deborah and I came together and will often start by saying that "I married a younger woman!" Folk's eyes normally grow larger, and I can only imagine what they are thinking. Then I say, "I am sixty-five and she was sixty-four and a half."

Now, I will share with you how Deborah and I became husband and wife. I had fallen in love with Deborah's mind, how she thought and spoke and processed things. I just loved her for that, first before anything else. And she had my heart by this time, completely. We were already married in our hearts and minds with no doubt. We consummated our marriage in private, prior to our public wedding ceremony, which we had later with family and friends. After several months of talking, sharing, getting to know each other's views on most things in life, we were both realizing that we were going to get married. I had even told Deborah, "I plan to wed you." She still chuckles about that statement because I used the old King James way of speech. Although I have no conscious remembrance of saying it that way, I mostly read the old King James Bible, so I am sure she is correct, and I did say it that way.

So, right in sync with our full disclosure to each other of our innermost thoughts, feelings and opinions, we also had wanted to know if we would be compatible sexually. Our kisses had been wonderful, our holding of hands had been full of energy and love. We had talked about so many things and were so very comfortable with each other in every way, we then wanted to proceed to intimacy.

On the day we first made love, there was more to the story before it happened. We were together, not planning to get intimate at all. Then, we looked at each other and both knew we wanted to be intimate. I looked Deborah in the eyes and said, "If we do this, there is no turning back. We are committing ourselves to each other for life. I don't want to do this unless we are both fully committing ourselves to each other. Are you okay with that?" That was certainly not the most eloquent or romantic proposal for marriage, but it clarified the commitment we were making to each other. We were standing there in the sight of God, and this was not a test, it was a commitment. She said yes. I said yes, and we had a private marriage, in His sight, with no preacher and no paperwork. Rather like when God presented Eve to Adam in the garden, or when Rebecca got off of her camel and went into Isaacs's tent. There was no recorded ceremony and no paperwork. So, it was with Deborah and me. And it was beautiful! From that day forward, we knew we were married. It was official in His sight. We do not apologize for the beautiful coming together we had in His sight. He was there, and we were committed. The paperwork and public ceremony were to follow three months later, as was a formal proposal too! Not the traditional order of things, that's for sure. And we are certainly not suggesting this as the way others should proceed. It is our story, and these were our decisions. You will have your own.

Shortly after this, I was reading my Bible and was exceptionally moved by the story of the prodigal son. I had read this story many times, but this time it was different. It touched me deeply. I have come to understand that my religious thinking was a form of sin. Binding me in a pathway which was destructive, and not in line with God's best plan for my life. When the prodigal son said, "I will arise and go to my father" his father ran to meet him and fell on his neck, had compassion on him and kissed him. He said nothing to his son that is recorded in Scripture. What is recorded is that the father spoke to his servants and said, "Bring forth the best robe and put it on him, and put a ring on his hand, and shoes on his feet: and bring hither the fatted calf, and kill it: and let us eat, and be merry: for this my son was dead, and is alive again, he was lost, and is found. And they began to be merry." Luke 15:22-24. (KJV). The part of the story which touched me most was when the father first saw his son coming, and he was yet a "great way off" the father ran toward his returning son. That is how I felt God moved toward me. He ran toward me when once

I started making the right decisions. I felt like the prodigal son during that three-hour prayer time with God when He flooded my heart with His care and mercy. I felt like He ran to me with his loving embrace. That is what God did for me when I woke from my religious stupor. He brought the very best to me, Deborah. A woman of great stature, kind, loving, intelligent, and my soul mate. The very best! While the eldest brother of the prodigal son complained about the compassion and forgiveness shown to his brother, the father said it is appropriate to celebrate. And so, it was with me, that God said it is appropriate for you to celebrate and I was again overwhelmed with his love for me in bringing Deborah and I together. It is amazing what God does when a person is honest and open in their hearts with Him and with themselves. When we are not imprisoned with rules and laws, but are seeking to be honest with Him in our hearts, God draws very near and reveals His love and care for us in wonderful ways.

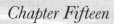

Chapter Fifteen

Surfer Dude & Surfer Girl

THE PROPOSAL

About a year before Deborah and I had committed to each other, I had planned a family trip to a beautiful resort area on the east coast as part of helping to heal family relationships. A place where famous folks had stayed in the past including royalty. A beautiful place. Originally, I thought that my ex-wife would accompany the family and had given her many chances to do so. She stated she would not go, and then when the divorce finalized, it cinched that. No way was she going. Now my dilemma was, should Deborah come with the family on this trip. We were privately married in His sight and in our hearts at this time, but what about the vacation with the family? There had not yet been a public wedding ceremony. As I prayed, I felt a very strong affirmation that it was appropriate for her to come. She would be in a position of honor, at my side. She had a hand in bringing the family back together. We were celebrating the family being healed in many respects. But what would the family think? Was it okay with them?

Deborah and I discussed it, and she said she would only come if it was acceptable with the family. I agreed and proceeded to ask each of them if they were okay with her coming. First, I asked my daughter. She said if it made me happy, she was all for it. Then my two oldest grandchildren, and they were delighted! I was surprised and grateful. As I asked each person, they all said, if it made me happy, they were fine with it. So, Deborah was going to come with us for the vacation! And then, I decided to make the formal proposal for marriage to her on that trip.

I had become friends with the pianist at the hotel during several school trips which I had coordinated in previous years for my grandkids. He was a very talented pianist and photographer and one of my "accomplices" in planning the proposal. When I called him to ask for his help, he was more than delighted to participate. We worked out the sheet music he would play, the timing, and things were set. The other accomplice was my son, who was going to secretly film and record the proposal.

Here was the plan. On the day we arrived, Jonathan, my friend and the pianist, would be in the dining room, at the piano, ready to start playing "Somewhere Over the Rainbow" as I started the proposal to Deborah. My son would arrive early and set up the recording equipment. Since the dining room opened for general seating at 5:30 in the evening, we would do this at 5:00 and be out of the way before opening. I would tell Deborah I wanted to show her the beautiful dining room, and escort her to the far end of it to an area known as the Queens Table, where Queen Elizabeth had dined many years earlier. This is where I would propose. Jonathan would start playing our song when he saw me get to the Queen's table. I think many places the Queen dined had a special area they promoted and named after her. Deborah was my Queen, so it was fitting for me to propose to her there. Everything was set. The problem was, I had forgotten how long it takes to drive to the resort from the airport. It became clear on the drive that it was going to be very tight to make it before the dining room opened. I was a nervous wreck on the last two hours of the drive. Deborah kept wondering why I was so concerned about getting there. She kept saying, "We will get there when we get there. No rush." We were caravanning with my son following us, my videographer and recording man. But right as we were entering a section of no cell phone reception, he took a wrong turn and was heading away from the destination! I couldn't call him. And I couldn't detour to chase him, or I too would be late. This will never work, I stressfully thought.

So, I planned to propose somehow, if I could just get there on time. About 45 minutes from arrival, a very slow line of traffic appeared before us. No passing lanes, no chance to speed up, and the clock was ticking. I was a wreck inside, and I know it showed. Now Deborah really wondered what was going on.

Somehow, we arrived just in time to get to the dining room at 5:00 p.m. on the button. And my son did too! He had recognized his error on the road, and quickly gotten back on the right one. As I was checking in, the general manager came out to say welcome. I had befriended him over the years on my previous trips. We were having a wonderful conversation, and I whispered to him that I was planning on proposing to my bride at the Queen's table and was late. He enthusiastically said, "Go man, go! I will make sure Jonathan is ready." He then said, "I proposed to my wife at the Queens' table too!" Wow! What a relief! And now I had the General Manager as part of the proposal team! How special it was and how wonderfully God had worked it all out.

As I walked Deborah into the dining room, Deborah was wondering why I wanted to show it to her so badly. I pointed out the windows, turning her gaze away from the piano, a beautiful Steinway Grand piano. I didn't want her to suspect anything was going on. We walked to the Queen's table area of the historic and beautiful dining room. When I reached the Queen's table, I turned to Deborah, took her hands, and began telling her of my love for her. As I did this, Jonathan began playing "Somewhere Over the Rainbow" on that beautiful Steinway! The melody magically floated through the huge dining room. Deborah looked at me, heard the song, and got teary eyed at what was happening. I continued the proposal, which took several minutes, and then, bending down on one knee, asked for her hand in marriage. Our previous commitment would not prevent the joy of a formal proposal. Her answer to my request for her hand in marriage was, "Yes! Yes! Yes!" Oh joy!!

One of my grandson's was watching from the entry to the dining room. He later told me that as I was proposing, he saw a dove fly by outside the window. A dove, the symbol of the Holy Spirit!

Our waiter that night for dinner had been commandeered by my son to film on a cell phone. He later shared with our table that he has been working there for many, many years, and it is moments like our proposal which are the things he will always remember as his most special memories. He was deeply touched by the proposal, music and planning. And the food was delicious!

Over the Rainbow

Our time there was magical. Wonderful hikes, great food and family fellowship. There was a bump in the road with my son, as he was going through his own adjustments to my new relationship and had his own issues as I shared. We made an effort to meet with him and his wife, which we did. We shared for a couple of hours and thought progress had been made. In the long run, things did not go well, and we will tell you that story later. He tried to disrupt my happiness and insert himself in his typical disruptive manner. Other than this bump, the entire week was wonderful and a blessing.

We have shared with you how Over the Rainbow became our song. I had learned it for Deborah, and we were certainly living in the reality of dreams coming true. More and more each day we are still living it. On one of our hikes, as we got toward the top, we turned to look down and there was a rainbow below us. We were physically above or "over" the rainbow. We have many pictures of this as we stood there in amazement and felt God's blessing and presence as He surrounded us with rainbows! It was phenomenal. This was no coincidence! It was the hand of the Creator, affirming our love and relationship once again. It is quite common to look up in the sky at a rainbow. But how many times are you actually above one, looking down at it? We were experiencing a very special moment, and we knew it. It is a blessing to allow God to be recognized in the little things that touch our lives. He fills the most common things with His love and presence when He is acknowledged. I have hiked that trail many times with no rainbows, so I know this was His hand blessing us.

Chinese food and God

One evening early in our courtship, Deborah and I were having dinner with my daughter and her family, and one of her daughters and her family at one of our favorite Chinese restaurants. Our grandkids enjoyed each other at dinner and had a lot of fun. Our kids connected and discovered they had common close friends. Deborah and I enjoyed the evening immensely, and all seemed to have a great time. It was at this dinner that my daughter reminded me that I had shared with her what God told me when I was twenty years old, "You will have many children." My daughter said, "Dad, this was what God meant!" Wow did that resonate in my heart!

My daughter later shared with us what happened as she was driving home with my grandson from that dinner. My daughter told me of my grandson's comments to her on their way home which were along these lines: "Mom, this is really of God. I have never seen grandpa so happy. God is really in this, Mom." Now we have heard one example of how good things can come from the mouth of babes. Well, my grandson sure saw God in my relationship with Deborah. He was ten years old at the time. He is also the one who said he saw a dove fly by the dining room window as I proposed to Deborah. I love it when God talks to kids! They can be so open and accepting of Him and His ways.

The Jail Cell Bars

On our last day at the resort, Deborah was sharing her concerns about her daughters' reaction to our getting together, and how quickly we were forging our relationship. Each had expressed concern to some degree and wanted the best for Deborah. She had been in two very difficult relationships, and they were worried. We had this conversation as we sat outside the hotel, looking at the grandeur around us. We were going home the next day, and Deborah's heart was troubled about her daughters. As she spoke, I had a vision from God. I saw her daughters in a four-sided jail cell outdoors on the ground, which was dirt. It had no roof, and each of the four walls was a wall of bars, like in the old west movie jail cells. As she expressed her concerns, I saw all four walls crash to the ground. They did not fall to the ground, but swiftly and forcibly crashed to the ground, dust flew high in the air form the impact, and her daughters were no longer constrained by the bars. That was it. I shared this with Deborah. I had no idea exactly what it meant. We were very soon to find out.

The next day we were driving home on the freeway. Of their own volition, each of her daughters called her to say hello, and to wish us best wishes in our engagement. They wanted to know if we would come over for champagne to celebrate our getting together. Her oldest daughter welcomed me as her new Dad, expressed delight about Deborah and I getting married, and had me in tears on the freeway. Not very safe, but surely a blessing! Tears were streaming down my face. This is the daughter who had previously come to me and Deborah and expressed Christian concerns about our coming together prior to a formal marriage. We were able to share with her our perspective and decisions, which we shared earlier in this book. She accepted our position, although I am not sure she agreed with it. However, she was very touched that we would open ourselves to her for this conversation, hear her concerns and position, and share ours. It was a very warm conversation, and we were all blessed. I think it was healing in some ways for everyone, as we avoided contention, loved each other while accepting each other's differing views. Later, I learned of how appreciative she was that I would sit down and talk with her. She had not been able to do such things with her real dad. That certainly warmed my heart! It is beautiful how God restores the years that the locusts have destroyed! Joel 2:25 (ESV).

DEBORAH THE PROPOSAL AND OLD TESTAMENT WEDDING

Things moved quickly between Kirk and me after we started dating. We went to his condo at the lake and committed to each other. I knew that he was to be my husband and I had no doubts.

We consummated our union. I was worried it was too soon, but it turned out to be a special part of our relationship. We were sixty-five and sixty-four at the time. Mature lovemaking is amazing!!!

My daughters and grandkids loved Kirk. All except for one grandson who had reservations when he found out Kirk's grandson was one of his best friends. He did not want to interact with Kirk. That passed and he and Kirk have a very close relationship. My daughters needed a strong Dad and my grandkids needed a grandfather. Kirk has filled a missing hole in my family. He is grandpa to the grandkids and dad to my daughters.

We had bumps coming up, of course. I wish we could say we lived happily ever after like in the fairy tales I had read as a child. We were living happily in our relationship, but life events swirled around us.

Kirk owned a wholesale distribution business at the time we met. He had recently reconnected with his son, with whom he had an up and down relationship. He and his business partners had decided to have their kids work in the business so they could hand it down to them when they retired. The other two partners had already pretty much retired, and Kirk had most of the responsibility. He hired his daughter and son to come into the business. Then Kirk got his divorce and I showed up. This threw his son for a loop. We were so much in love, and we both knew we were going to get married.

Kirk had been planning to take his kids, their spouses and grandkids on a family vacation for over a year. He invited me to go. I hesitated and told him he had to get permission from his kids. They said yes. So, six weeks after we started dating, I went with the family on the vacation. Kirk had planned to propose to me there, but I didn't know it. Kirk's son was going to help record the proposal. We were driving in a caravan and his son took a wrong turn. Kirk couldn't get ahold of him on the cell phone, and he was very stressed. I didn't know he had a proposal planned at 5:00 p.m. His friend, who was the pianist had helped set it up and was planning to be there at 4:30. Timing was critical, but I had no idea. I said, "We have plenty of time." Kirk said dinner was at six. We arrived at the resort, checked in, and went to our cabin.

Kirk said he wanted to show me the dining room and wanted to do it right away (I couldn't figure out why). Remember, he is a romantic. We strolled through the large room and ended up at the end in a spot called the Queen's table. (Queen Elizabeth had dined there years before.) As we stood there, I heard the piano player start to play "Over the Rainbow" by Izzy, our song that Kirk had learned just to sing to me. The piano player was a friend of Kirk's. Kirk had gotten to know him from taking his grandkids and their school groups there for years. It was the song Kirk had learned to sing just to me when we were getting to know each other in our coffee meetings! I went "Oh, Oh!" Kirk then proposed to me. I was so surprised and excited, and I said, "Yes, Yes, Yes!" I know it was early and sudden, but we both knew we were each other's soul mate. And his son had made it to the hotel on time and had a video and cell phone going that recorded the whole thing! We were so happy, and the family seemed to be.

But it turned out that his son was <u>not</u> happy. He threw a fit and we spent two hours that evening talking to him and his wife. He was mad about how Kirk had handled his wedding to his second wife and his divorce from his first wife. The trouble was just beginning. I should have seen it coming, as he tried to ruin our happiness that day.

The rest of the stay was fun. I got to know his family and even his son was civil to me. I watched Kirk and saw what a wonderful father and grandfather he was. Kirk and I decided to set a wedding date. I wanted to get married at this special resort and we were looking at November of that year, seven months

away. It was all booked up except July 2nd was open, and my
siblings could all be there. It was very unusual for this time to be
available, so it had to be the Lord holding it open for us. We set
the date and ordered invitations. There was no doubt in my mind
that I wanted to spend the rest of my life with Kirk. We knew
what we wanted, we were ready and why waste time at our ages???
Unfortunately, it was a little too soon for his son and daughter.
They had not adjusted to the divorce (even though they supported
Kirk in it) and they were not ready for him to start a new life. My
daughters were thrilled that I was marrying Kirk, and they had
already had years to adjust to my divorce.

THE WAR BEGINS

Kirk's son was still angry, even though he had hidden it, and his
ex-wife wanted the marriage stopped. They called Kirk's best
friend and his sister and told them horrible lies about us and our
relationship. It ruined Kirk's relationship with his best friend and
his sister was very wary. Then, Kirk's daughter was not happy with
Kirk because of some work issues and his son wasn't even going
into work. Kirk decided to reduce their capacities and lowered
their salaries a few weeks before the wedding. Well, a hurricane
broke loose. They met at Kirk's office and the son came in yelling.
I was there. They both verbally ripped Kirk apart, Kirk then
relented and left them both with their high salaries for a little
while longer. He would take care of this after the wedding. I think
some of this was their reacting to their dad's divorce and getting
remarried so quickly.

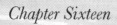

Chapter Sixteen

Surfer Dude & Surfer Girl

KIRK--THE WEDDING

Our wedding was magical. We planned it at a beautiful resort. It was overlooking a scenic lake. They had just completed a remodel and addition of a beautiful banquet area. Because they wanted to show off their new facility, we got very special attention. Guests came from all over to attend, and many stayed at the resort. In family guest rooms the chef prepared a beautiful fruit, cheese and meat tray that was amazing. The food was over the top delicious, and everyone had a great time.

Deborah and I had all of our kids and grandkids in the wedding. All but one, who was sick after a trip to the east coast. As we were preparing for the ceremony, Deborah and I were to not see each other until the event. Well, as it happened, I was in the elevator going down to the wedding, when the door opened Deborah and the bride's maids were all standing there to get on the elevator. It was an amazing fun moment, and quite a surprise! All the girls giggled. She was stunningly beautiful, and still is!

I can still remember standing up front with the pastor when Deborah walked into the room with her father. She was so elegant and amazing, that picture of her is seared in my mind! And her father, ninety-seven at the time, walked her down the aisle, with a little help from Deborah. Four of our kids sang at the ceremony, bringing us to tears.

When it came time for the outdoor photos, as we were walking back inside, the sunset became epic with amazing bright colors, clouds, and silhouettes of the forest. Our photographer grabbed us and said, "Quick, get up on that rock outcropping!" We did, and he guided us into an embrace where I held her in my arms, bending over and leaning her almost to the ground, with this sunset going off all around us. It was like a scene from Gone With The Wind. The photo is so beautiful it looks like it was photo shopped.

DEBORAH— THE WEDDING

We had a beautiful wedding at a special resort in a newly remodeled event space. Our grandchildren were all in the wedding and the five kids participated in the wedding. (My son did not attend even though he had been invited). My siblings and their families and my father and stepmother were also there, as well as many friends. My ninety-seven-year-old father walked me down the aisle. It was an amazing ceremony centered on God, as He had brought us together. We had three days of celebrating in a beautiful spot with amazing food and music, friends, and family.

We went on a honeymoon to Hawaii and bought a condo, so that Kirk could surf, and we could both snorkel and swim. This was to be a big part of our retirement. Kirk and I love the ocean. We were even circled by two small sharks while I was on a paddle board and Kirk was swimming, but that didn't dissuade us from being in the water. We were being blended and combined into each other with God's hand on us. His blessings were abundant.

Back home, after the honeymoon, we reveled in our lives as husband and wife. Kirk included me immediately in his finances as we joined both of ours together. We had a magical time at the lake kayaking and stand-up paddle boarding. Many evenings were spent watching sunsets and paddling over to a little cove for a sunset dinner. We were staying at my house, and we started to clean out his house he had been in for seventeen years. This was a special time as we started our routines and rhythms of life with each other. God was very central in all of this. He even gave Kirk a song about me called "My Deborah". We were finally in a relationship that included God and that was one of positivity and encouragement.

Chapter Seventeen

Surfer Dude & Surfer Girl

OUR SONGS AND INTIMACY

Our Songs

We have shared how I learned Izzy's "Somewhere Over the Rainbow" to sing to Deborah. We have been blessed so many times with that song since then. Most recently we were walking back from a stroll along the beach in Hawaii near a beachfront restaurant with entertainment. We sat on the shore in a comfortable love seat provided for that purpose and watched a Black Crown Night Heron hunt in the surf for his dinner. As we sat there, the stars were shining, the trade winds blowing, and for the first time we actually saw this bird catch a fish. We had watched them many times before, stoically freezing in a posture ready to strike, but they never did. The one he caught was so large we thought there was no way he could swallow it. It took several minutes, but he managed to slide it down his throat. That must have lasted him a week.

Well about an hour later, as we were about ready to leave the love seat, the Hawaiian beach guitarist began singing "Alleluia", a song we had our four children sing at our wedding. We looked at each other in amazement. Then, right after this, for his last song of the night, he sang Izzy's, "Somewhere Over the Rainbow." How special. And we were very blessed by the Lord in those moments. No one else was with us on the beach; only the two of us, the Lord, and the Black Crowned Night Heron. (And the fish he had caught, but they were in his tummy by this time.)

My Song for Deborah

My heart was so full of love and thanksgiving as Deborah and I embarked upon our life together, that I told her I wanted to write her a song, but nothing came. My feelings were there, overflowing, but I could not get words or a melody. I drew a blank for several months. Then one night I was playing the keyboard, and the song came like a flowing river. Here are the lyrics.

My Deborah, my angel love.
Sent to me from God above
My Deborah, my angel love,
Sent to me in His love.
He looked upon our heart's desires
Saw the paths we'd walked alone
Said that I will make them one
They shall know my love
He saw the pain, saw the need for healing
Knew that we would make each other whole
As it was in the very beginning
So fresh, so new so pure.
Now he makes all things new

> In His love secure
> Oh, such love I've never known
> Till there was you,
> Till there was you, Deborah,
> Till there was you
> My angel love.

I sing it to her often! It is so true how He looked upon the two of us. Saw that even though we had been in marriages, we had mostly walked alone. He saw our pain, He knew we would be good for each other, and somehow in His grace and love He said, "I will bring them together!" What a wonderful God we serve!

DEBORAH-INTIMACY

We both had some wounds sexually from our previous marriages. The sexual union is very important in a marriage, and it is important to the emotional and mental connections of the couple. There is a debate in counseling literature as to whether the relationship affects the sexuality or vice versa. I think it is both. Kirk and I love to touch each other, whether it is affectionately or sexually. I love how he smells, kisses, and feels. He treats me with respect and love outside of our bed and in our bed. He is very attentive and will open my car door for me and give me a kiss before we go anywhere. Kirk watches out for me and makes sure I am okay no matter what we are doing. He pays attention to me and my body during love making, and I pay attention to him and his body. We hug and cuddle for quite a while after lovemaking. We connect with hugs, kisses, and touching often during the day and even touch each other during sleep. Our previous sexual wounds are forgotten. Previously, I was treated as an object and would not want to be naked or partially unclothed around my ex, as he would want to have sex whether I wanted to or not. I learned to avoid my ex. I feel safe and open with Kirk and am comfortable when unclothed. He is safe for me. We match in our bodies and in our sexual rhythms.

Kirk is a surfer, and he makes love like a surfer on a wave. He is able to feel the movement of my body and match it to his. We become one. Prov 30:18-19 "Three things are too wonderful for me; four I do not understand: the way of an eagle in the air, the way of a serpent upon a rock, the way of a ship in the midst of the sea, and the way of a man with a maid." (KJV). This is Kirk, my surfer dude.

Kirk's ex-wife was not interested in being sexual and in fact had mostly refused to engage in intimacy for the last seven years of their marriage. I was open to him sexually and this healed his wounds.

Communicating is vital for sexual intimacy. We tell each other what we like and what feels good sexually. We also speak up about what we do not like. The other part of intimacy is the emotional and communication aspect. We go to each other when we have an argument or are upset with one another. We are open to saying, "I'm sorry and please forgive me." And then we forgive each other. This is amazing for me also, as I never heard those words before!!! I don't think Kirk did either. This soothes the soul and helps us to move together through life and to remain connected spiritually, mentally, emotionally, physically and sexually.

Chapter Eighteen

Surfer Dude & Surfer Girl

ISSUES WITH FRIENDS AND FAMILY

KIRK - Partners, Sister and a New Man

When my business partners of thirty-five years heard my story and saw my new happy self, they commented that they had never seen me so happy. They rejoiced with my newfound life and relationship with Deborah. They wished me all the happiness in the world.

My sister said the same thing. She said my voice over the phone sounded like a totally different brother. A really happy one! She was right. And she said she was very happy for me and had a better perspective of my past marriage trials than I realized. She had seen more of the difficulty I endured than I ever realized. I was the blind one, but those around me saw it clearer. Our conversations were immensely comforting.

I forget who said it, but one of my friends or my sister said that my mother, if she was still alive, would be very happy for me.

I think that was one of the most moving things anyone said to me. I know she would have loved Deborah. They thought so too.

Casualties of Divorce & Discovering True Friends

Divorce brings with it some casualties. It is a breaking apart of a relationship, and just as a large rock dropped in a calm lake creates ripples, so does a divorce. Others around us feel its impact to some degree. The rock and the water feel it most, as they are at the point of impact, and then those closest to us feel its impact, and those farther out are less affected. None the less, divorce affects our family, our friends and our acquaintances. And it is not all happy. Not everyone rejoices in our newfound happiness and relationship. Here is a brief account of some of the negatives which occurred to Deborah and me.

My ex-wife, and my son, while expressing positive statements to me personally, were very active behind the scenes saying all manner of evil things about me to my best friend and my sister. What I learned was being said, I learned much later. And when compared to what they said to my face, it was shocking to learn of their bitterness and venomous statements. I guess I was very naive. They dared not speak to me, for some reason, but sure told tales to others. They spun lies about Deborah and I having an affair prior to the divorce, saying that we must have been planning this for a long time. This was not the case, as we did not have our first date, or our first kiss until after my divorce was final. Our relationship did move along fast, but not prior to my divorce. Deborah never came into focus for me until after I decided for sure to get a divorce. My ex was telling me how re-connected she was with my best friend's wife, a very unlikely story. My ex had terminated a relationship with her many years before and did not like her. She was fabricating lies about them both getting together soon, and how wonderful it was to reconnect. They never spoke again to my knowledge and never got together. But it was clear that my ex had maliciously inserted herself with my best friend to hurt me. At least that is my take on the motive.

After my ex dumped her lies on my best friend, he called me a "manipulative swine" for the way I had assisted my ex-wife getting out of the hospital. Really? Supporting her own demands to be released is being a manipulative swine? Trying to get her to stay in the hospital another night because the hospital nurse thought it was best is manipulative? Getting mad on her behalf to get her home was wrong when this was her vehement demand of me? Then, while to my face my son was saying he was so happy for me, and if it made me happy to please bring Deborah on the vacation, he was telling others how terrible it was, and expressing a totally opposite story to them. In the world of psychology, this is called triangulating. Drawing others into your anger and resentment behind the back of the one you are not willing to confront directly. It is very destructive when the person drawn in doesn't see the whole picture. Some folks are downright masters at triangulation. I think my son is one of them. My best friend supported their venomous position without even asking me what was really going on. I was shocked. He was a casualty of the divorce for sure. And still is. This is my long time "airport encounter" friend. It is still sad to think about losing this friendship.

My sister bought into my son's story line, going back to my son's perceived wrongs many years ago as a result of his divorce. My sister was very empathetic with my son and had sided with him without ever knowing the truth nor the whole story. However, she eventually, not too long after, came around after hearing "the rest of the story" as Paul Harvey used to say. Today, I do have a good relationship with my sister. And I am grateful for that! My son took this opportunity to plead the victim in his own divorce and paint me as the villain for seeking the best for his two children. I had previously wanted to get past the tear in my relationship with my son, so much so, that I had reached out and apologized for things I never did wrong. This patched things up for the moment but backfired soon thereafter. I was learning that you cannot continue in relationship with a person full of resentment and bitterness until there is a change in the person who is causing all of the pain and attacking. To my son, I was the one to blame for all of his problems. This was more of what had been going on for years, particularly since my son's divorce, where I sided with his ex-wife for the sake of the children. He had consistently done things that were not good for them.

In many respects, my son treated me like he saw my ex treat me. If it was not a learned behavior, it was at least encouraged by what he saw my ex-wife do. I had put up with my wife's verbal abuse for so long, I guess my son thought it was ok to treat me like she did. My son's texts, emails and conversations were often venomous, and hate charged! It would turn my stomach, and I could feel physically the impact of his attacks.

Fact is, when folks have issues, whatever they may be, a divorce can unearth them with great force and impact. We learn who our real friends are, the unconditional ones who are friends through good and bad, thick and thin. This book is not about the many issues that can be unearthed, that is for another day.

My experiences with all of this helped me learn to set boundaries. If someone conducts themselves as an attacker, or ridiculer, or harasser, they are not allowed in my life. I have stopped trying to fix other people's issues. If someone has constructive criticism, I welcome it. But hate spawned conduct and words are not ok, no matter who they come from. It is not my responsibility to fix others, which is their personal work. It is enough to take care of myself!

One of my other long-time good friends and his wife did nothing but celebrate our happiness, joined us in the wedding and celebrations, and remain close friends to this day. Wonderful! My cousin and his wife were another couple who offered nothing but joy and support for me and Deborah. Even though we had not kept in contact much over the years, they rejoiced with us, attended our wedding, and are to this day a great blessing.

True friends stick with you through all things. Judgmental ones are painful. Both family and friends can be affected by skillful triangulation. Sad but true.

DEBORAH - OUR NEW LIFE AND INTERACTIONS-LIFE'S DYSFUNCTIONS DON'T DISAPPEAR QUICKLY, OR LIFE'S MISTAKES? ADJUSTING TO A NEW LIFE.

After a few months of marriage to Kirk, one of my daughters wanted to buy my house, so we moved into Kirk's house. (The grandkids ages fourteen and sixteen asked me first to buy the house!) We helped my daughter upgrade her existing house in order to sell it and helped her to afford to buy mine. Kirk's ex was a bit of a hoarder and we cleaned out truckloads of items that she had left behind in his house. We donated at least a thousand light bulbs and many doo dads. I must have found forty clocks and seventy blankets!

While Kirk and I were fine and content, Kirk's kids were not. Kirk's son continued to not show up for work, and both of his kids were being negative. Kirk's daughter was angry at her dad and the work relationship still wasn't working out. Kirk fired her. Then he fired his son right after Christmas, and he went on a rampage with emails and texts attacking both of us. So much for family togetherness. The relationship with Kirk's son was cut off, and he was not able to have contact with his youngest granddaughter. This had happened before with the son, and Kirk was done with his anger and attacks.

Then Kirk hired a new Controller. The company accounting was a mess, and it appeared to look like his previous Controller had embezzled 1.2 million dollars. The Controller had to hire all new staffing and to figure out the very complicated accounting system. This was a very stressful time for Kirk, and also for her. There was no embezzlement just sloppy accounting.

As 2017 began, we went to Hawaii for three months and Kirk worked remotely. It was our plan to spend about half the year in Hawaii and half at home. He surfed and we snorkeled and swam and enjoyed our time together. Things seemed to quiet down. We had our honeymoon time! We explored the island and had many adventures together. Kirk's business pressures were there daily to deal with, but he was able to handle it. I didn't have to hold him up emotionally! He handled his own emotions and stresses. I was there to support him, but I did not have to be codependent. Whew!!!

When we returned home to the mainland, we decided to look for a new house or lot to build on. Kirk drew a floor plan we both liked. We decided against building and started looking at existing homes. We found nothing and decided to remodel the home that Kirk had from his divorce. The remodeling estimate was too expensive. Then, God told Kirk to "Look". So, we did. Lo and behold our realtor called us, and we found the perfect house which was almost exactly the floor plan that Kirk had drawn. We bought the house, moved in, and went to Hawaii for three weeks. Our other house sold two weeks later as we were hiking in a volcano. We returned and started settling into our new home. God was leading us into a totally new life.

BUMPY ROADS WITH ADULT CHILDREN

I had been divorced for eleven years at this point, and my children were adjusted to the divorce and my new marriage, I thought. Kirk's children, on the other hand, really had had no time to adjust to his divorce and our remarriage. They were in their forties and were very aware of how difficult his previous marriage had been. But – the divorce and remarriage had to be processed by the adult children. In August of 2017, Kirk had another upset with his daughter. We took a break for a few months and then met to discuss the issues with her and her husband. We prayed with them first. His daughter was able to air her upset at the divorce and at issues she had with Kirk. The conversation got heated at times, but we hung in there. We all resolved the upset and there has been a new establishment of a healthy relationship with Kirk's daughter and her husband. God was very present in that conversation.

In any healthy marriage or relationship, it is vital to have open conversations. Neither Kirk nor I had experienced that in our previous marriages. We were not allowed to express ourselves. But now, Kirk and I could talk openly about issues between us and also, we could talk openly to our adult children. To be able to share without being told basically to be quiet was new for me and also for Kirk.

But the upset with other adult children continued at Christmas. I thought my children were all fine with my new marriage. But new rules had to be established. My son came home for Christmas after four years of not showing up and of course did not want to see me. My ex was also in town, and that created upset for my daughters too. It was all about how they could spend time with us and also with my son and ex. We somehow made it through Christmas, but my daughters and grandchildren were exhausted, and we were very hurt. We went to Hawaii with heavy hearts. We were able to talk it through later and come up with some new holiday plans. It is hard on adult children to juggle seeing their divorced parents and siblings on holidays. We all had to learn to share our time and to be supportive of how the Holidays are to be handled.

We didn't know that family issues were going to be something we had to learn to work through with our adult children. They were all reacting to our marriage and to the changes in their individual ways. Our marriage was sudden for everyone except us. We felt like we had always been together, as our minds and hearts were entwined. Kirk had a vision that our lives together were like a rocket ship taking off with parts falling off as we left the atmosphere and went off into space. We had lots of parts to let go of!!!!!

Kirk and I have been able to navigate the many issues since we got engaged mainly because Christ is at the center of our marriage. We go to Him in prayer about our decisions and our family. We read scripture daily and want Jesus involved. He leads us in unexpected ways at times. One of the things that we have learned to do is to make repairs as quickly as possible when we have had an issue, or something has come up with the family. Kirk is better at this than I am, as I still hesitate at times to confront issues for fear of conflict. A repair is made when the couple turns toward each other. If Kirk and I have an issue, we both immediately apologize for our part in it, hug each other and then discuss what happened. Sometimes it is just that one of us is tired or stressed or that we are reacting to something outside of our relationship. Turning toward each other instead of turning away keeps us connected. John Gottman and Nan

Silver, *The Seven Principles for Making Marriage Work*, (Harmony Publishing, 2015). If it is an issue with a family member, we try to discuss it with that person. With healthy people, conversation can occur that will resolve the issue.

BUSINESS STRESSES AND TRAVEL

2018 was a difficult year for Kirk's business. Kirk had been semi-retired for a couple of years, but at times the business would draw him back to nearly full-time work. Our marriage even affected his business! He was tired of the day-to-day management and his two partners had retired. His interests had a new focus – being married to me and enjoying a new life and relaxing. Changes were happening. But God was in control of the business also.

Kirk and I were growing closer and were enjoying each other more and more. We had discussed planning trips and traveling while we were still physically able to enjoy it. We spent three months in Hawaii and went to New Zealand for two weeks in the middle of that time. We spent most of the time there at Mount Manganui, where Kirk got to surf, and I enjoyed the beach and beach town. We met a family friend of mine and her husband. We drove to a famous surf spot and then went up to the Bay of Islands. There was lots of rain and lots of fun.

After returning home, we went to Israel in April for two weeks. That trip changed our lives, as we saw where Jesus lived, walked, died and was resurrected. We felt his presence on that soil and especially at the Sea of Galilee. We met some Christians from Africa and joined them in prayer on the shore of the Sea. It was amazing to see some of the first century synagogues which had been excavated, and where Jesus probably preached. Jerusalem was also very touching, as we visited the Old City and the Garden. Kirk was an amazing fellow traveler. So different from traveling with my ex who constantly caused upset and conflicts. Kirk and I were able to relax and enjoy the new experiences.

The problems with Kirk's business continued and were awaiting us on our return from our travels. Things weren't going well at the company, as the managers were slacking off.

Summer came with some highlights and some low points. Our relationship was solid, but we had outside issues going on, including the weather! There were lots of forest fires, and the lake and home were blanketed in smoke. We tried to stay at the lake but got sick from the smoke. With a smoke haze hanging over us, we had a birthday party for Kirk and family members in July (a tradition of Kirk's) at the lake. Not only did we have smoke, but we had fire as one of my daughters was upset at us for helping the families unequally. It took a while to resolve the upset over the next week, but we were able to work through it. We learned a big lesson! Giving unequally caused hurt and pain for all of us. We also learned to not be so involved in our kid's finances and to let God be the one to provide for them. We are all still adjusting to new family rules.

"Where no oxen are, the crib is clean; but much increase is by the strength of the ox." Proverbs 14:4. (King James Version). Where there is family, there will be trouble at times, but it is worth the energy to have the strength and blessing of the family. It is so amazing to be able to work things out with adult children and grandchildren. The ones who have accepted Christ as Savior are forgiving and gracious.

God has continued to bless us and our family. We have two "missing" children who do not want to be in relationship with us and we have accepted this. Our other four adult children and grandchildren are precious and wonderful. The interactions are mostly positive, and we are able to be supportive as the elders.

We and the family have made it through the adjustments of our marriage and now have a great relationship.

Kirk was able to lead my one-hundred-year-old father to the Lord that summer – a highlight. My father had been in and out of the ER and hospital all year. God told Kirk what to say as we drove over for an ER visit. He was going to march into his hospital room, talk to no one else, and tell my father he was going to accept Jesus as his Savior. Somehow, I knew what Kirk was going to do. Knowing my dad, <u>telling</u> him was required! God knew how to reach my father. He told my father about Jesus and that he needed to accept him, and my father prayed the prayer in his own words. It turned out there was nothing wrong with him physically and he was discharged later that day. God caused him to not be able to stand or move so that Kirk could witness to him. We praise God for that!!

Chapter Nineteen

Surfer Girl & Surfer Dude

DEBORAH - TRAUMA AND DRAMA AND REDEMPTION

2019 started our quietly, but it soon erupted. Kirk, in his efforts to retire like his other partners, expanded the duties of his partner's son to include the management of the entire company as the other managers were slacking off. Both managers quit within a month. Two months later, Kirk notified the father, Kirk's partner, that numbers were way down, and his partner's son immediately resigned. Kirk was left with a newly hired operations manager and a budget way out of line for the operations, and everything back in his lap. We had been in Hawaii for the winter and returned to this commotion. Things eventually worked out amazingly well, but this experience was very trying for Kirk.

And my issues with my family of origin (father and all siblings) were heating up. As a reminder, the cycle in the home that I grew up in was an abuse cycle. Abuse (I hate you), honeymoon period (I love you), a calm period then tension (criticism, resentment), abuse... My sisters, brother, Dad and I have always been enmeshed, and not in a healthy way. Enmeshment is defined as a relationship between two or more people in which personal boundaries are permeable and unclear. Boundaries are invisible psychological fences that define where people begin and end. There were no clear boundaries between me and my siblings, nor my father. We were too close emotionally, and we have been intertwined in an unhealthy way. As my mother had died in 1981, my father remarried in 1982. His wife never opened up to me and her boundaries were closed. She has been very distant. Healthy boundaries are ones in which the communication lines are open for positive interaction and closed to negative interaction. If negative interaction occurs, the people involved with healthy boundaries are able to talk it out and resolve issues. Unhealthy boundaries cause conflict, hurt, strife, and pain. My family had unhealthy boundaries. Henry Cloud and John Townsend, *Boundaries* (Zondervan, 2017).

God's next rocket part that he was removing from our marriage was my enmeshment with my father, my brother and sisters. In March of 2019, my father had been put in the hospital for a UTI and was in rehab for six weeks. We arrived home from Hawaii when he was in rehab. I had been the only child mainly involved for the last fifteen years. I had been present with him for multiple ER visits, hospitalizations, surgeries, and long rehab stints. I was continuing in this role when my siblings decided to boot me out and take over his care. All the old family dynamics resurfaced, and it became very ugly. My siblings still worked under the old rule that you could rip someone apart verbally and then be loving friends the next day. We continued to visit and spend time with my dad, but we stepped back to avoid as much family drama as we could.

My work with God, and what He was doing in my heart

began to separate me from my sisters, my brother and my father emotionally. I visited my dad every ten days or so to continue to honor him. The Lord has helped me establish healthy boundaries with them all. Unhealthy old family patterns can only be broken by Jesus. He breaks the intergenerational dysfunctional family patterns. He is the ultimate transitional figure, as He changes our hearts and minds. He also can use us to be transitional figures, as He changes our behaviors and attitudes.

At one point, between the business chaos and my drama with my family, I told God I could hardly cope with much more. Then God intervened!! Out of the blue Kirk received an offer from a large company to buy the business. Kirk initially said no, as the last two years had poor profits and there had even been two capital calls. They persisted and Kirk accepted the offer to sell the business. Kirk had seven months of hard work ahead of him to complete the sale, and I was praying for Kirk! God kept His hand on Kirk and the sale went through!

KIRK – SALE OF THE COMPANY

As you now know from earlier in our story, the companies God gave me an interest in, we kept and operated for 35 years. As the partners all got a bit older, including me, there were some tensions between us. We had tried for several years to bring our children into the business to keep it going into the future. We had also attempted to sell the companies a few years earlier, and the offers were simply too low to justify selling. It was much better financially to keep them and run them. Well, things got touchy, and began to stress a very unique and successful 35-year partnership. And most of the tension came from our kid's involvement. Family loyalties take priority over partners. Damage was being done, not only to the partner's relationships, but also to many of the long-term employees of the company, and the financial future of the companies was in jeopardy. It was not good. It was so stressful that I felt it could likely end in litigation and fighting among the partners in the not-too-distant future.

After operating through two very poor years financially, we received an unsolicited offer from three different buyers. It came to me through the Broker we had used to try and sell the companies a few years earlier. I told him, no, we are not interested in selling right now because we just came off of two very poor years. He said the buyers don't care about that; they wanted our operations and locations in their portfolio. I shared our sale price range, and said if they can come in that range, we can talk. Well, the broker said that range was ok with the buyers. I then said, great, let's talk.

The first company flew out their top guys the next day, we met, and two days later they made a solid offer! We haggled a little, and all went very smoothly. We were having productive talks with two other potential buyers, but once the first offer got into shape, we were required to stop discussions with all others during the due diligence period, to which we agreed.

The companies sold seven months later. For the complexity of the sale, this was seven months of hard work for me, but things went amazingly smooth the entire time from offer to close of escrow. It was truly from God! Little did we know at the time that the decisions our government would make because of Covid-19, would shut down the economy. Had we still owned the business operations, we would have been devastated, and likely would have had to put one of the companies into bankruptcy! The buyers had resources to carry them through a business slowdown, which is what happened. The buyers had to nearly close all of the operations we had sold to them. God spared us from all of that. He is amazing and His timing is wonderful. I remember when

I was praying about the business before Deborah and I were married, God had told me He was going to bless the business. I had no idea what He meant and preserving it to be able to sell it was a huge blessing!

DEBORAH

The sale of Kirk's business closed in November of 2019. The rest of the year was spent with Kirk finalizing the sale and us enjoying our kids and grandkids. We also spent lots of time deciding how to invest, as this would be our only income as we were now both fully retired.

How did Kirk and I handle all this change? We did a lot of praying and relying on God to guide us. The Bible in Romans 8:28 (ESV) says God works all things to the good for those who love Him and are called according to his purpose, and it is true!

Chapter Twenty

Surfer Girl And Surfer Dude

DEBORAH - 2020 – THE CRAZIEST YEAR

God told me at the beginning of the year, "I'm in charge, not you." I was still thinking I had to be responsible for my family's and Kirk's wellbeing. My codependent tendencies still were popping up. God is in charge, and I keep reminding myself of this because 2020 has been a crazy year. By now we had been married for three and a half years. If we had taken a stress test on all the stresses, we would have been off the charts. Divorce, marriage, adult children's issues, selling two houses, buying a house and a condo, Kirk's business stresses, my issues with my dad and siblings, and then selling Kirk's business would have put us over the top. But God had His hand on all of it as He worked in our hearts and minds to stop the old unhealthy patterns. We had come through it all because we were able to communicate openly, support each other, repair any upsets, and be flexible with our new life and changing rules and patterns. To lean on God is amazing, as He has His plans, and He is in charge.

We went to Hawaii in January and the three oldest granddaughters came over the next day. After the granddaughters left, we were settling into our routine in Hawaii. We had no idea what was about to hit.

Around the first of March, we started to hear about the Coronavirus 19. It was spreading quickly in Europe and was showing up on cruise ships. By the first of April the United States was closing down. People were panicked as the media talked about mass deaths and overrun hospitals. Our freedoms were slowly taken away. It started out as "Shelter in Place and be careful when you are out". Then news reports came out about how infectious it was. It seemed like in a day the country shut down and we were told to Stay at Home. We had to cancel the other six grandchildren's trips to Hawaii. We had been bringing them over three at time for special grandparent time for a few years. We enjoyed exploring, snorkeling, belly boarding, kayaking, and Kirk was able to teach them how to surf and arranged surf lessons for them. Most stores were closed except Costco, Target, Walmart and grocery stores. Beaches were closed as well as most parking lots. But we were told we could go in the water if you went in and out and did not stand or sit on the beach. Our beach parking lot remained open, so we were lucky. People couldn't congregate and groups of over ten were not allowed. Churches were all closed, and events were cancelled (including Easter services). It progressed to where you had to wear a mask to buy anything and in public people were not allowed to stand still. We had to keep a 6-foot social distance. VRBO rentals were all cancelled, and the hotels and resorts were closed.

God had certainly protected us. He sold the Kirk's company, as He knew this was coming! We would have been devastated financially. He also had us in Hawaii with all of this COVID-19, so that we could swim in the ocean and Kirk could surf. God blessed us with a weekly worship and fellowship with some Christian neighbors in our backyard in Hawaii starting on Easter. It was like the early church, meeting from house to house. God showered us with His blessings in the middle of Covid 19. We can't wait to see what He will be doing next!!!

DEBORAH

So, how have Kirk and I coped with all the changes and challenges of the last five years?

We have supported each other. Not that we are perfect, because we aren't. Kirk is very even tempered, but he will have an occasional outburst if he is too stressed. I will usually get quiet and want to keep to myself. I will become very upset if I am pushed too far. I have difficulty speaking up at times, and I am worried Kirk will react negatively if I speak up. We know this about each other and can give each other space until we can talk about it. We seem to be able to resolve conflicts pretty quickly. It is because we both listen to each other and care about the other person's feelings.

Jesus is the one who brings about heart changes. When a person accepts Christ as his savior and asks Him into his/her life, Jesus brings about character and other changes in that person's life. Jesus also needs to be a part of a relationship. He helps us to forgive each other and to move on. We both can say we are sorry when we are in the wrong. This needs to be followed by a change in behavior. God is slowly moving us from incorrect thinking into His thinking.

Both Kirk and I were mismatched in our previous marriages. We tried to be attached in a healthy, give and take way to our previous spouses, but they attached differently to us. Sometimes it is just a mismatch. Trying to cover a mismatch with Biblical principles easily leads to misery! Neither Kirk nor I were tough skinned enough to let the abuse pass over us. Instead, it got inside of our psyches, and it took both of us a long time to realize and recognize what was going on. We would have been spared a lot of heart ache and wasted energy if we had been able to be honest about our marriages. They were not of the heart after a period of time. They were marriages on paper and from the legality of the Christian church teachings that we were exposed to.

I believe that if people aren't married in their hearts, they aren't married and it is a sham, a pretending. A friend of our shared that God had told her the basic particle of the universe is love, and that is God. God knows our hearts and He loves us. He gives us grace and understands us. He wants the best for us and doesn't want us to be dishonest in our relationships and in our marriages. He really loves us!

My marriage to Kirk has been what God intended marriage to be. He has had His hand on both of us for many years and brought us together when the time was right in His eyes. We wish we had met when we were young, and that we could have had children together. But that is not what happened, and we both were being formed by God for His purpose in other circumstances.

KIRK

In Ephesians chapter five, we are shown the way God intended for marriage to be. The husband is to love his wife, as Christ loved the Church and gave Himself for her. And the wife is to respect and honor her husband. This is what Deborah and I have entered. It takes both spouses to want this for it to work. I yearned for a fulfilling relationship my entire life, but it was never fulfilled. I want to honor, respect, cherish and care for Deborah, and she in return wants to honor, respect and care for me. She is delighted by my caring for her, as I am with her affection toward me. She receives my love warmly and is grateful for it. As I am for her love. Because we both want this relationship, and desire it to work, it does! When only one partner is committed to this type of a relationship, it simply will not work. When one partner has personality disorders, or emotional issues, it easily prevents a marriage from becoming what God intended. Facing the reality of a relationship which cannot function properly is a big step in moving forward with one's life. I had refused to see the brokenness of my first marriage for too many years. I always thought it would get better, or that it was my calling to endure for the rest of my life. Having now tasted of the beauty of a healthy marriage, I can see my errors more clearly, and wish I had exited sooner. Sometimes, as Deborah mentioned in her story, it is simply a mismatch. And it is worth repeating, when you try and cover over a mismatch with Biblical principles, it can lead to long term misery.

The Lord has more than restored the damages of the past in my life. He brought Deborah to me, the greatest gift of my life! We are allowed to spend time in Hawaii, where I can still enjoy surfing, kayaking, snorkeling and the surrounding beauty, and share all of these things with Deborah. We have been given many new friends, and a wonderful church family in Hawaii. God has been so good to us! It was truly like we were on the back side of the desert for many years, and then God led us into the Promised Land! We made it! It just took us a lot of years.

A Whale Tale

We enjoy kayaking in the ocean and often paddle out several miles from shore following the whales. We have a two-person pedal kayak, and Deborah sits in the front seat, and I sit in the back. We have seen breaches very close to our kayak, one so close it was scary, as we thought the whale would land on us! On another occasion, a baby whale and its mother were swimming around us for quite a while. We were just sitting still watching them a good distance away. Then the baby surfaced right in front of our kayak, and with its side fin extended it and gently bumped the side of the bow of our boat as if to say, "What is this thing?" It then swam away as the mother whale surfaced right next to the baby. The gentle bump rocked our kayak a bit. It was an amazing experience.

So, as we end our story, we would like to share some thoughts with you about whales. When we go out in the kayak sometimes, we will end up three to four miles offshore as we see spouts and follow the whales. Sometimes we will be out for hours and see nothing, or only in the distance. Sometimes we will sit quietly and wait for one to come by. We have thoughts about our relationship with God and the whales. So here are some thoughts we have developed.

The whales come and go from Hawaii in their season. They are not there all the time. God visits us in seasons and sometimes seems farther away, like when the whales are up in Alaska. But He is always with us, sort of like the whales are always in the ocean.

The whales have great senses, and they know where we are, although we do not always know where they are. They are very powerful, and if they wanted to, they could destroy our little boat, or land on it in a breach. We see them for only a few minutes at a time normally, and they are out of sight the rest of the time, but they are still down there. God is very powerful and could destroy us in an instant if He so chose. He is also very sensory, and knows everything about us, and where we are in our hearts and minds, and physically. God seems to appear to us in brief moments, and then for extended periods of time He seems silent, or not visible in a situation, but He is always there.

Sometimes we will hear the whales singing in the water, but we cannot see them. That reminds us of the Holy Spirit being with us every day, "singing" His comfort and guidance even though we cannot see Him. We need to be quiet and still to hear the whales and to hear God. The whales seem hidden most of the time, sort of like God seems to us at times.

God is magnificent, and so are the whales. When one breaches next to you it takes your breath away. They are so huge, and yet so coordinated, like the story we shared about the baby whale gently bumping the front of our kayak. When God appears to us from his "hiding place" it takes our breath away, He is so magnificent, loving, merciful and powerful.

Sometimes we only get to observe the whales from a distance, a mile away or so. And then suddenly one can be right next to you, surfacing for air or breaching. God at times is seen only from a distance, but then when we least expect it, He can be very close.

Sometimes we will spend hours on the water and see nothing at all. However, the more time we spend on the water, the more likely we are to see a whale. If we don't put our kayak in the water, then we won't have any encounters with whales for sure. This is similar to our seeking God. The more time we spend in His presence in prayer, reading the Word and worship, the more likely we will see Him and understand Him. If we don't spend any time in His presence, then we won't experience Him very much at all.

We must get out on the water and search for the whales to find them. If we stayed on the shore, we would never have a close encounter with them. We must search for God to find Him, as He says that we will find Him when we seek Him with all of our heart. Sometimes we need to just be still and wait in His presence, like sitting on the water waiting for a whale to pass by. And often they do, and often He does too.

Having a hunger to search for God is a gift from Him.

SOME THOUGHTS FOR THE READERS

We wrote this book in hopes that it will help other couples define their marriages. We hope this will help those in fixable marriages improve their marriage relationship. It is our hope that those in destructive marriages will be able to find a way out. The ultimate goal would be for each person in the relationship to look honestly at the relationship and their part in it. We recommend strongly that if a marriage is struggling, get professional help from a counselor trained in Marriage Therapy, preferably with a Christian focus.

If the marriage is a mismatch, then professional help should also be sought to see if the relationship can be salvaged and made whole, or if it is too detrimental for all involved to continue the relationship. We both wish we had been honest about how miserable we were in our previous marriages. Maybe by being honest, the marriages could have been saved. Or the honesty would have brought out the truth, and lots of pain could have been spared for all the parties involved, including the children. Two of our children were casualties of the unhealthy marriages and our parts in them. We both stayed in the previous marriages even though we were not married in our hearts to our ex's, and it was very difficult. We stayed faithful, but we weren't being honest about how we were living.

We have a list of questions we would like both people in the marriage to ask themselves. This is for an honest assessment of the marriage.

Marriage Diagnostic Check List: What is broken or needing to be worked on in your marriage?

1. Do I keep from sharing with my spouse how I feel or what I think because of past negative reactions when I express myself?
2. Do I repeatedly find myself in a negative state of mind or depression or hopelessness, because of continued behavior patterns with my spouse?
3. Do I think about suicide as a way to relieve the pain I feel?
4. Do I feel at times like leaving and never coming back?
5. Do I make excuses for neglectful or abusive behavior in my spouse?
6. Have the issues that cause me pain and frustration continued, and I have not been honest with myself about them? Have I expressed my feelings and thoughts about these issues to my spouse? Am I realistically accepting the facts, or am I ignoring them, or excusing them?
7. Is what I am going through destructive to me, my children, or others in the family?
8. If I am honest with myself, am I being verbally abused? Emotionally or mentally abused? Physically abused? Sexually abused?
9. Do I have a good sexual relationship with my spouse? Do I want one? If not, why not?
10. Is God whispering to me the truth of my situation and I am ignoring His voice?
11. Does one person always blame the other, or others in their life for their own personal issues, consequences or failures.
12. Does one person not treat the other with respect?
13. Does one person abuse the other verbally, mentally, emotionally, physically, sexually? Is there constant

belittling, diminishing comments, threatening language or actions, mental manipulation?

14. Does one person not take responsibility for their shortcomings/actions?

15. Does one person fail to see any reason to change, and in fact does not change in any positive way. (Beware, that for short periods of time some may change, but shortly thereafter return to the negative/destructive previous behavior.)

16. Does one person find they are accepting/taking the blame for everything, even when in their heart they know this is not correct?

17. Does one person in the relationship never say they are sorry, with heart felt sincerity?

18. Does one person retaliate with personal attacks instead of accepting and working on the issues? "You are so stupid." "It is your fault I because of this or that."

19. Does one person always criticize?

20. Does one person always become defensive?

21. Is there substance abuse present? Is there an addiction to pornography, gambling or any other addiction?

After you each answer these questions honestly, we hope that you can see clearly to honestly evaluate and accept the actual condition of your marriage. And if professional counseling would be helpful, that you will seek it. And it is critical to ultimately honestly answer the question, "Should I Stay, or Should I Leave?" God knows your heart and being honest with Him is the place to start.

Bibliography

American Psychiatric Association. "What is PTSD". Accessed November 7, 2021. https://www.psychiatry.org/patients-families/ptsd/what-is-ptsd

Evans, Patricia, *The Verbally Abusive Relationship*. Avon MA: Adams Media, 2012.

Gottman, John M., and Silver, Nan, *The Seven Principles for Making Marriage Work*. New York: Harmony Publishing, 2015.

Healthline.com, "Fight,Flight, Freeze: What the Response Means", Accessed November 7, 2021. https://www.healthline.com/health/relationships/cycle-of-abuse

Healthline.com, "Understanding the Cycle of Abuse", Crystal Raypole, November 29, 2020. Accessed November 7, 2021.

Hemfelt, Robert, Minirth, Frank and Meier, Paul, *Love is a Choice*, Nashville, Tennessee: Thomas Nelson, 2003.

Shapiro, Francine, *Eye Movement Desensitization and Reprocessing*, New York: Guilford Press, 2018.

Printed in the United States
by Baker & Taylor Publisher Services